P9-DTR-571

FOREVER YOUNG:
THE 'TEEN-AGING' OF MODERN CULTURE

Marcel Danesi

The excessive worship of adolescence and its social empowerment by adult institutions is the deeply rooted cause of a serious cultural malaise. So argues semiotician Marcel Danesi in *Forever Young*, an unforgiving and controversial look at modern culture's incessant drive to create a 'teen-aging' of adult life.

Written for the general reader and based on five years of interviews with over two hundred adolescents and their parents, Danesi's book begins by asserting that one of the early causes of this crystallization of adolescence as an age category can be traced back to theories of psychology at the turn of the twentieth century. Since then, the psychological view of adolescence as a stressful period of adjustment has become a self-fulfilling prophecy. This, in tandem with the devaluation of the family by the media and society at large, has led to a maturity gap – a fissure in family dynamics that is eagerly and ably exploited by the mass media.

Unlike many academic digressions into the malaise of modern culture, *Forever Young* provides concrete answers on how the 'forever young syndrome' can be addressed. One solution is to dispel the myth that experts and professionals are the people best equipped to give advice on raising children. The second is to recognize the value of family, in all its different combinations, as the primary institution of child rearing. The third is to challenge the pervasive notion that teen culture is a sophisticated endeavour – that, for example, pop music can claim to have produced some of the best musical art in the world, surpassing Mozart or Bach.

By laying bare the misguided tenets that have brought about, and continue to promote, a 'forever young' mentality, Marcel Danesi demonstrates that the 'teen-aging' of culture has come about because it is, simply put, good for business. Teen tastes have achieved cultural supremacy because the Western economic system requires a conformist and easily manipulated market, and has thus joined forces with the media-entertainment oligarchy to promote a deterministic 'forever young' market.

MARCEL DANESI is a professor of Semiotics and Anthropology at the University of Toronto.

MARCEL DANESI

Forever Young
The 'Teen-Aging' of Modern Culture

UNIVERSITY OF TORONTO PRESS
Toronto Buffalo London

© University of Toronto Press Incorporated 2003
Toronto Buffalo London
Printed in Canada

ISBN 0-8020-8851-1 (cloth)
ISBN 0-8020-8620-9 (paper)

∞

Printed on acid-free paper

National Library of Canada Cataloguing in Publication

Danesi, Marcel, 1946–
    Forever young : the teen-aging of modern culture / Marcel Danesi.

    Includes bibliographical references and index.
    ISBN 0-8020-8851-1 (bound)   ISBN 0-8020-8620-9 (pbk.)

    1. Adolescence – Social aspects.   I. Title.

    HQ796.D352 2003   305.235   C2003-901726-5

University of Toronto Press acknowledges the financial assistance to its
publishing program of the Canada Council for the Arts and the Ontario
Arts Council.

University of Toronto Press acknowledges the financial support for its
publishing activities of the Government of Canada through the Book
Publishing Industry Development Program (BPIDP).

Contents

Preface

In January 1995, I was a guest on a nation-wide CBC radio phone-in program, talking about the potential implications that the portrait of adolescence I had painted in my recently published book, *Cool: The Signs and Meanings of Adolescence* (University of Toronto Press, 1994), had for society at large. Most of the callers seemed to enjoy my responses and comments to their fairly straightforward queries. Towards the end of the program, however, a caller from Vancouver asked me something that caught me off guard. She queried, 'Is not the portrait you are painting of adolescence a consequence of a larger tendency in our society for people to think of themselves as forever teenagers?' I had no ready-made answer to give her. I do not recall how I got around her question, but I am pretty sure that whatever I said did not satisfy her. I know for certain that it did not satisfy me.

What a terrific insight, I thought to myself on the way home from the studio. That perceptive caller had put her finger not only on the probable reason why adolescence has become such an all-encompassing social problem but also on a deeply rooted cultural malaise – the excessive worship of adolescence itself and its social empowerment by adult institutions. She challenged me, in effect, to dig deeper below the cultural terrain to unravel the causes of what may be called the 'teen-aging' of modern culture. As I contemplated the many ramifications of the caller's question, the highly popular 1984 pop song 'Forever Young,' by the group Alphaville, came to my mind. Its lyrics are revealing: 'Let us die young, or live forever ... Forever young, oh, to be forever young.' The subtext of that song is a transparent one – to save the world it is necessary to cling to the idealism of youth, so as to avoid the moral corruption that comes with aging. What a romantic view, I thought! Why is it so widespread? And why has it led to fundamental changes in the socio-logical structure of the modern world?

My reason for writing this book is to attempt answers (or at least responses) to such questions and, thus, to provide a meaningful answer to my Vancouver caller's challenging query. In so doing, I beg the reader's indulgence because, at times, I will be quite blunt in assail-ing some of the sacred cows that are nowadays accepted as principles of 'common sense.' One of these is the deeply ingrained notion that 'experts' and 'professionals' are the ones to whom we must turn for advice in raising children. In truth, the horde of psychiatrists and social workers trained to provide such advice know little more than what instinct and intuition can already tell us. A second notion is a corollary to the first – namely, that the 'experts' can step in, if need be, to replace the family in the business of child rearing. I must emphasize from the very outset that there simply is no 'science' of rearing children, no 'right way' to raise the young! As with other animals, rearing is some-thing that comes instinctually to human beings. It is simply foolish to believe that society's behavioural and social scientists can replace the family in matters of rearing. A third notion concerns the perception that pop music – especially rock and roll – has produced some of the best works of musical art of the modern world. In my view, pop music is fun art, not profound art. How can anyone even think of comparing jazz, rock, and rap pieces to the works of a Mozart or a Beethoven, as many music critics now do on a regular basis? There is absolutely nothing in the pop-music repertoire that comes close to the profundity of Mozart's *Requiem Mass* or Beethoven's Ninth Symphony. Yes, there are some truly wonderful jazz, rock, and rap works around. I mention, for instance, the compositions of the Platters, the Beatles, Procol Harum, Pink Floyd, the Moody Blues, and Nirvana. But, frankly, how comparable are they to, say, Mozart's *Don Giovanni* or Verdi's *Rigoletto*?

My goal is to lay bare the misguided tenets that have brought about, and continue to promote, a 'forever young' mentality. It is irrelevant to me whether people agree or disagree with my observations. I am con-vinced that the time has come to dispel the romantic myth of 'young is good, old is bad' that fuels virtually all the engines of our market econ-omy. The subtext on which I will develop my case is that the 'teen-aging' of culture has come about because it is, simply put, good for business. Pop music, for instance, has become the norm because trends within it pass quickly from the teen world to the adult world and, thus, can be sold and recycled over and over to all age groups. Moreover, since teen tastes change virtually overnight, instant obsolescence can be built into the creation, marketing, and promotion of the new music trends. This guarantees a quick turnover of products. The same kind of ephemerality has been built into practically everything else, from clothing fashions and cosmetics to television programming. Teen tastes have become the tastes of all because the economic system in which we now live requires this to be so, and it has thus joined forces with the media-entertainment oligarchy to promote its forever young philosophy on a daily basis. In a phrase, youth sells!

The field work conducted for this book (consisting of more than 200 interviews with adolescents and parents) was supported largely by two grants: one from the Social Sciences and Humanities Research Council of Canada and one from Victoria College of the University of Toronto. I am grateful to both. Although it is based largely on the findings of the field work, I must stress from the outset that this book is not directed primarily at an academic audience. The topic is too important to be discussed only within the confines of academia. Nevertheless, many of my comments have a scholarly ring to them. The subject matter of this book cannot really be presented in any other way without diluting it to such an extent as to make it superficial.

I should, however, make a commentary here on how the data for this book were gathered. Through the grants, a number of research assistants were hired at the University of Toronto in 2000, 2001, and 2002 – Karatina Kuruc, Kate O'Neill, Kate McGee, Biagio Aulino, Tracy Tam, Dominika Solan, Stéphanie Belanger, Pinella Buongiorno, Lindsay Kochen, Katie Lauder, and Marianna Calamia. They were instructed to tape spontaneous conversations of teenagers interacting socially. They were then asked to follow up this phase with interviews with the teenagers, utilizing questions related to the main areas of concern to be treated in this book: why they dress the way they do, why they listen to the music that they do, how they relate to parents, and so on. No 'standard questionnaire' was used because it was thought that this would 'stilt' the interviews with teens, who typically are wary of such social-scientific methods. The researchers – all university students trained in cultural analysis – were told what kind of specific information was needed. It was left up to each one to get it in any way he or she could in response to the 'interpersonal dynamics' of the specific situation. Follow-up interviews were also carried out by the researchers with the parents of the teenagers. The parental perspective on why teens look, talk, and act the way they do, and what they think about it, is of obvious importance to the subject matter of this book. Information of this kind was collected in nine North American cities (including Toronto, San Francisco, and San Diego) and in several areas of France, Slovakia, and Italy. All the information was taped and then fully transcribed. Parental and teenager consent was sought beforehand. This 'open ethnographic' research method produced, surprisingly, very rich data, although it did leave inevitable gaps for quantification purposes. However, since the primary aim of this book is to draw a portrait of an endemic cultural mindset in a general way, the lack of 'statistical control' of the data has not diminished the overall pertinence of the portrait. At least I hope so.

I wish to thank the many people who have helped me, influenced me, and critiqued me over the years. First and foremost, I must thank the myriad of students I have had the privilege of teaching over the last thirty years at the University of Toronto. They have always been a constant source of stimulation and enrichment. Without mentioning names, I wish to thank the numerous reporters and media personalities who provided me with insights during the interviews that followed the publication of *Cool*. They apparently felt that I had a great deal to say to the public at large, and encouraged me to do so. I must mention the constant advice and help I have received over many years from Professor Frank Nuessel of the University of Louisville. I am also truly grateful to the editorial staff at University of Toronto Press, especially Bill Harnum, Kristen Pederson, Ron Schoeffel, Anne Laughlin, Len Husband, Frances Mundy, Margaret Allen, and Melissa Pitts. The Press is a leader in matters of social concern. I agree, however, with Bill that I took too long in getting this manuscript completed. I hope that the result was worth the wait. Finally, a heartfelt thanks goes out to my family – Lucy (my wife), Alexander and Sarah (my grandchildren), Danila (my daughter), Chris (my son-in-law), and Danilo (my father) – for all their patience with me during the research and writing phases. I truly must beg their forgiveness for having been so cantankerous and heedless of family duties.

I dedicate this book (and any royalties it may garner) to Child Find. My heart goes out to those families with missing children.

FOREVER YOUNG:
THE 'TEEN-AGING' OF MODERN CULTURE

CHAPTER ONE

The Fountain of Youth

The pursuit of happiness, which American citizens are obliged to undertake, tends to involve them in trying to perpetuate the moods, tastes and aptitudes of youth.

Malcolm Muggeridge (1903–1990)

In April 1994, I was attending an academic conference in the city of San Francisco. One evening, a colleague approached me with an invitation to accompany him to a Jerry Garcia and the Grateful Dead concert nearby. I hesitated at first; but then I decided that it could be quite entertaining, or at least very interesting, to see an icon of counter-culture rock and roll perform live on stage, even though he was way past his creative prime. After all, I thought, the Dead were best known for their live performances, which featured extended instrumental improvisations that never failed to excite audiences. The Dead were the stuff of legend. Their frequent concert tours earned them legions of devoted followers, known as Deadheads, many of whom became social activists, living a free-spirited, alternative lifestyle, with no particular plans for living other than to follow the band from concert to concert. They would be there for certain and, I thought, it would be interesting to revisit a rock and roll 'happening,' as it used to be called in the hippie 1960s. So, I accepted the invitation. As it turned out, that was one of Garcia's last public appearances. He died shortly thereafter of an apparent heart attack at a California drug-rehabilitation centre on 9 August 1995. He was fifty-three years old.

During the performance, I noticed a mixture of very young and rather old Deadheads in the audience. One particular pair of fans caught my eye – a boy around thirteen years of age who was grooving to the music alongside a woman who was (I estimated) in her early seventies. As I could see from their body language, both Deadheads were really 'into the music,' as they used to say in the 1960s. The woman's attire matched that of the younger Deadhead. She wore scruffy jeans and a T-shirt with a picture of Garcia on the front and the phrase 'The Dead Are Alive and Well' on the back. Only the colour of her long hair – pure white – and the craggy physiognomy of her face gave concrete indications of her age. At first, I viewed this as a rather quaint picture of modern times – young and old united by 'good old rock and roll.' Once a Deadhead, it would seem, always a Deadhead. But as the pair continued grooving to the interminable song droning on from the stage, the scene before me started taking on a dissonant quality. Something was not quite genuine about it. The more I thought about it, the more it jarred me. That rather pleasant-looking woman had never grown up, I concluded. She had drunk from the 'fountain of youth' a long time ago, and she was still feeling the after-effects of its magical water. Having totally lost interest in the white-haired, over-weight Garcia and his attempt to bring back the past with his wavering voice, his hollow-ringing hippie lyrics, and his counter-culture attire (complete with mandatory T-shirt and jeans), I left the theatre long before the concert ended.

I quickly put that event out of my mind until January 1995 when, as mentioned in the preface, I received a call during a phone-in radio program that brought back the image of the seventy-year-old Deadhead, along with the questions that her presence at the concert raised for me. Was she simply there to have fun with a grandson; or was she holding on desperately to her youth? Was she, in fact, an unwitting victim of a widespread general tendency in society at large to worship and hold on to all things youthful and fun? I sensed that the latter was the case. But if so, then how did this 'forever young' mind-set come about? And is it related to our culture's obsession with adolescence? The goal of this book is to seek plausible answers to these two questions. This opening chapter constitutes a historical point of departure to my quest.

Childhood

Puberty – the point in the life cycle when an individual becomes phys-iologically capable of reproduction – is nature's way of ensuring the continuity of our species. The advent of this critical biological point in an individual's life has always been celebrated in traditional societies in some ritualistic way. The celebration is known as a 'passage rite,' because it inheres in the enactment of a set of customs that are designed to mark in a communal way the 'passage' from childhood to adulthood and to signal the social responsibilities that this entails. In city-based cultures, even in the ancient world, however, passage rites lost their importance as communal events, being assigned primarily to the religious sphere, where they continue, in fact, to be important – I mention the Catholic sacrament of Confirmation and the Jewish Bar Mitzvah as two cases in point.

In all previous eras of Western history, the period before puberty held no special significance. Children were prepared for work as soon as it became physically possible for them to carry out chores. Children as young as five tilled the fields, milked cows, gathered hay, and tended to animals. There was little, if any, distinction between child-hood and adult work roles. There were no idyllic novels or poems written about childhood; nor were there special laws, customs, or prac-tices related specifically to the rearing of children. That remained the status quo (more or less) until the Industrial Revolution of the nine-teenth century when, in cities throughout Europe, more and more chil-dren were put into schools rather than sent out to work the land or carry out agricultural chores. To be sure, many city children were also expected to go out and work. But, unlike the farm, the new industrial workplace was an inhospitable one. In the early factories and mechani-cal shops, children simply could not keep up with the pace or carry out the type of labour required of them. As a result, they were treated with harshness and barbarity – a brutal situation that has been imprinted indelibly into our collective memory by novels such as Charles Dick-ens's *Oliver Twist* (1838). Within a short time, specific laws were passed to protect children. It became illegal, for example, to send children out to work before the age of maturity. At about the same time, romantic writers started depicting childhood as a period of 'innocence' and 'fan-tasy.' Inspired by Jean-Jacques Rousseau's novel *Émile* (1762), which may have been the first literary work to fashion an idealized image of childhood, writers such as Robert Louis Stevenson (*Treasure Island*, 1883) and Rudyard Kipling (*The Jungle Book*, 1894) started spreading a new 'fantasyland' view of the pre-pubescent period. By the early part of the twentieth century, this utopian view had become firmly implanted in cultural groupthink, and reinforced by works such as Sir James Matthew Barrie's *Peter Pan* (1904). Barrie's novel was converted into an extremely popular Broadway musical (1954) and Disney movie (1953), and continues to spawn emotionally powerful descendants such as Penny Marshall's 1988 movie *Big*. However, the fantasyland view of childhood does not exist in many other parts of the world, nor do the laws to safeguard and preserve it. Indeed, it is estimated that the number of what we in the West define as 'working children' is in the hundreds of millions worldwide.

The nineteenth century also produced a new 'scientific' view of childhood. Influenced by social Darwinism, the early practitioners of psychology (then in its infancy) claimed that children underwent adaptive stages of mental and emotional growth as predictable as the stages of bodily growth. This became such a widespread and dominant idea that, to this day, it is felt to be beyond reproach. It is one of those deeply entrenched concepts that we no longer realize came about as controversial and unfounded conjectures. As I have discussed elsewhere, humans cannot be studied with scientific methodology.[1] Human behaviour and development vary extensively with each situation and are not predictable. The so-called stages that psychologists talk about are dependent almost entirely on the situation in which a child is reared, as the Russian psychologist L.S. Vygotsky argued throughout his brilliant career in the early part of the twentieth century.[2] In earlier eras, the stage of crawling, for instance, would hardly have been seen as the 'psychological milestone' it is today. In the medieval period, crawling on the floor was viewed as animal-like behaviour and, consequently, as something to be corrected. Children were thus clothed in attire that kept them in a rigid, adultlike posture that forced them to stand as early as possible.

The merging of our fantasyland and scientific views of children has had a profound impact on the cultural, economic, and institutional fabric of our society. For example, as anthropologist Helen Fisher observed a decade ago, these are what impel human parents today, unlike the parents of other primates, to 'continue to rear their offspring some ten to twelve years after these children have been weaned.'[3] There are now more laws protecting children than there are laws protecting adults. There are more books written for or about children than there are on virtually any other topic of human concern. The toy industry has become central to our economy. Take dolls as a case in point. These were hardly considered to be things for little girls to play with prior to the nineteenth century. Dolls were intended for mature women, either as *objets d'art* or as 'miniature fashion models' on which to put new clothing styles for display. The idea of giving dolls to children to play with came about, *ipso facto*, as a consequence of the fantasyland view of childhood. Children have always played with objects and continue to do so, from broom handles to pebbles (which can be imagined to be swords and valuable jewels, for instance). But manufacturing toys on a massive scale for children would have been considered preposterous before the 'reconceptualization' of childhood that took place barely 150 years ago.

Coming of Age

Needless to say, many good things have come out of the fantasyland view of childhood. As never before, children today are protected against abuses of all kinds; literacy in childhood has become a right, not a privilege; children are probably happier now than ever before; and so on and so forth. But like any artificially created concept, it has also had negative consequences, of which the most significant is, in my view, the extension of childhood to beyond puberty – an extension that, as I will argue throughout this book, has benefited absolutely no one. This extension comes under the rubric of 'adolescence.'

After industrialization, it became obvious that a literate workforce was needed. For this reason, children were expected to go to school, rather than work. As the new workplace expanded and became more sophisticated, so too did the need for workers with higher levels of literacy. So, children were kept in school longer. That event radically changed the course of Western history. It created modern-day adolescence.

The term *adolescens* was used in the Middle Ages to refer to any prepubescent boy who decided to move away from the family farm to work independently in some guild or trade.[4] For the next five centuries, this meaning remained virtually unchanged. Late in the eighteenth century, an event took place in England that radically altered this definition of the term. It was called the Sunday school movement – a movement that was conceived initially for the benefit of poor and working children. It laid the foundation for the possibility of mass education. By the time of the Industrial Revolution, education for one and all became a practical necessity. In response to the new situation, the children who stayed in school beyond puberty were called *adolescents* – a usage that stood in obvious distortion of the original meaning of the word.

From the outset, 'adolescents' were trouble – at school, at home, and in society at large. And the reason why – sexually mature individuals cannot put their sexual urges on hold in order to concentrate on school as they did when they were children – was simply ignored. Adolescents were subsequently refashioned as 'older children.' To make sure that sexual urges did not get the better of these 'older children,' complicated taboos were created; and these were quickly incorporated into law. But Mother Nature could not be denied. The new 'restraining measures' brought about many unwelcome repercussions – an unprecedented growth in the rate of unwanted pregnancies, a frightening increase in the incidence of sexually transmitted diseases among adolescents, and the emergence of youth gangs that allowed the adolescents to set themselves apart from adults, to mention a few.

To rationalize the appearance of such problems, a new 'theory' of human development during adolescence was needed. The psychologist Stanley G. Hall (1844–1924) provided such a theory opportunely in 1904.[5] Known as 'recapitulation theory,' it was, in hindsight, a rather simple and rhetorically persuasive one; but it was totally unfounded. However, it was just what the social doctor ordered. Hall postulated that the development from childhood to adulthood constituted a kind of Darwinian 'recapitulation' of the evolutionary forces that characterized the development of the human race. Accordingly, the infant 'recapitulated' humanity's animal stage, the adolescent the savage stage, and the adult the mature (sapient) stage. Predictably, Hall went on, the passage from one stage to the other is a difficult one, for the reason that 'transitions' require adaptation and adjustment. Undoubtedly, Hall's theory would have been quickly discarded as the fanciful speculation of an overactive academic imagination if not for the fact that society desperately needed it as a rationalization (if not justification) for having called into existence the 'problems of adolescence.' The theory legitimized two things at once – adolescence and developmental psychology itself. Shortly after Hall's proposal, Sigmund Freud (1856–1939), the Austrian physician and founder of psychoanalysis, put forward another convenient theory. Following on Hall's coat-tails, Freud claimed that adolescents were troublesome creatures because their childhood experiences made the adjustment to adulthood 'traumatic.' Incredibly, Freud's preposterous proposal, which initially met with the hostility that it deserved, made its way into the mainstream. Although later psychologists, such as Erik Erikson, attenuated his notion somewhat by pointing out that cultural factors other than childhood 'repressions' play a role in adolescence, Freud's theory has nevertheless become an intrinsic part of our groupthink.[6] The contemporary version of trauma theory goes somewhat like this. Inhabiting a strange, new, sexual body, adolescents start to feel awkward, anxious, and guilty (or afraid) of their desires and feelings. Consequently, they are besieged by a pervasive awareness of, and sensitivity to, what others think of them. Membership in a peer group is their way of gaining shelter from the ravaging effects of 'growing up.' The peer group serves, therefore, as a kind of asylum from the burdens of puberty.

Trauma theory is known more colloquially as *Sturm und Drang* theory (German for 'storm and stress'). It is convenient, but ultimately useless.[7] This can be seen in the fact that clinical psychologists have failed to deal in any effective way with solving the more serious problems of adolescence. Simply put, the storm and stress symptoms that we assume to be typical of adolescence simply do not emerge in cultures that have never extended childhood into the pubescent years – and there are a significant number of them around even today. Already in the late 1920s, the great American anthropologist Margaret Mead (1901–78) had assembled a large corpus of data on a non-Western society – the Samoan one – which showed rather persuasively that the purported traumatic experiences of North American adolescence were symptoms of a stilted cultural experiment. Mead reported that Samoan children followed a smooth, continuous growth pattern, with no apparent Freudian traumas at puberty.[8] Culture, not nature, she maintained, had created the conditions that fostered such traumas.

But despite Mead's efforts to dispel the *Sturm und Drang* view of adolescence, it was simply too convenient a rationale for coming to grips with the problems of adolescence. By the end of the First World War, adolescents came to be viewed by society at large as maturing children requiring special handling at home and at school. We have been living with the repercussions of this view ever since. In 1939, the term *teenager* appeared for the first time in a magazine article. That was the year after the Fair Labor Standards Act in the United States set the minimum age of fourteen for employment outside school hours. In 1944, *Seventeen* magazine began publication, indicating that adolescence had emerged as a social and economic force to be reckoned with. By the mid-1950s, the adolescent population had become a vital sector of the economy, at the same time that the behaviour of teenagers was becoming increasingly more worrisome to parents and educators. Psychology came, once again, to the rescue. It reassured parents that adolescence was nothing more than a 'passing' phase – a term expressing more of a wish than anything else! Since then, the number of books on this passing phase has reached astronomical proportions. Adolescence is not only good for the economy; it is also good for academia.[9] The number of professional organizations that have sprouted up to deal with the problems of adolescence is mind-boggling. Their names are self-explanatory and tell a frightening story on their own – the National Youth Gang Center Institute for Intergovernmental Research, Students against Drunk Driving, the National Parents Resource Institute on Drug Education, Teens Teaching AIDS Prevention, the National Youth Advocacy Coalition, Covenant House, the National Runaway Switchboard, the National Youth Crisis Hotline, the National Association of Anorexia Nervosa and Associated Disorders, and the list could go on and on.

But, one may ask, why would Mother Nature have gone so far out of her way to wreak such havoc upon her sexually maturing human progeny? The answer, as Margaret Mead made plain decades ago, is that she has not.[10] Adolescence is a difficult phase in modern life because we have made it so by artificially extending childhood beyond puberty. And its age boundaries are being constantly expanded. To wit: social adolescence now starts before puberty and lasts way beyond it. It is not unusual, in fact, to find pre-pubescent children today, as young as seven or eight, manifesting all the hallmark signs of adolescence. They now even have a name: *tweenies* ('in-betweens'). And, needless to say, there is an increasing tendency among some (perhaps many) individuals to extend their adolescent lifestyles well into their twenties and even thirties. The term *middlescent* was coined by American journalist Gail Sheehy in the mid-1990s to refer to such individuals.[11] Tweenies and middlescents, incidentally, have become clearly distinct 'market populations.' The tweenies, for instance, now have their own TV shows (such as the Disney Channel and YTV), stores (Betwixt in Greenwich Village), and snacks (Hot Bites, a line of frozen miniature pizza and potato snacks from Heinz).

The largely uncontested view of adolescence as a stormy and stressful period of life constitutes, in effect, a case of a self-fulfilling prophecy. By making school obligatory during the pubescent years, by passing specific kinds of labour and family laws for the protection of adolescents, by targeting them as a market segment, by defining them as 'half children, half adults,' by pampering them, and by expecting them to defer the responsibilities of social adulthood until after the high school (and even college) years, we have brought about the social conditions that favour and sustain the peculiar (and often unwanted) behaviours that we associate with the modern adolescent period. This situation has even had an effect on Mother Nature herself. In the 1970s, puberty was documented as beginning two years earlier for girls in the West than it did in the early part of the twentieth century! Culture, it would seem, has nature by the tail.

Juvenilization

The notion of adolescence has not only provided a rationalization for keeping sexually mature children artificially 'on hold,' it has also been a godsend for the economy and our media–entertainment industries. The image of the teenager as a rebellious figure – sexually mature but emotionally and socially childish – has been a source of limitless capital for book and magazine publishers, recording companies, Hollywood, and television since at least the 1950s. As a consequence, the notion of adolescence has become itself mythologized by the media. Trends in the adolescent world quickly become the cultural norm, dictating look, taste in music, and fashion for the simple reason that they are everywhere. Juvenile aesthetics are now the aesthetics of all. I will refer, henceforward, to this general tendency as *juvenilization*.

The roots of juvenilization can be traced to three sources: (1) to the truly marvellous advances in medicine and health-care delivery at the turn of the twentieth century that made it possible for people to live and remain healthy for much longer than ever before; (2) to an unprecedented increase in the spread of personal wealth at about the same time that made it conceivable for more and more people to indulge in the material accoutrements of the modern world, including fashion and cosmetics; (3) to the disempowerment of the family in matters of courtship and maturation (who and when to marry, what job or profession to pursue, where to live, etc.). With more wealth and leisure time at their disposal, and without the strict controls of the traditional rural family, common people became more inclined to live the good life and to decide on their own whims whom to marry, what jobs to pursue, and so forth. Such trends were entrenched and nurtured by the messages that bombarded society from radio and print sources in the early part of the twentieth century – messages that became more persuasive and widespread with the advent of television as a social force in the early 1950s. By the 1960s, the desire to be young meant the desire not only to stay and look healthier for a longer period of one's life but also to act and think differently from 'older' people. Being old meant being a part of the corrupt and morally fossilized 'establishment,' as the consumerist way of life was called by the counter-culture dissidents of the era. By the end of the decade, the process of juvenilization had reached a critical mass, on the verge of becoming *the* defining feature of Western groupthink. As the social critic Stuart Ewen has aptly put it, the business world discovered fortuitously in that era how to incorporate the powerful images of youth protest into 'the most constantly available lexicon from which many of us draw the visual grammar of our lives.'[12] What appealed to the young would shortly thereafter appeal as well to the old. It became a collective state of mind.

Needless to say, a society bombarded incessantly by images of youth is bound to become more and more susceptible to seeing those images as the norm. Because our consciousness is shaped by the type of stimuli and information to which we are exposed, the barrage of images, generated by the media, of young, beautiful, fun-loving people surreptitiously influences communal lifestyle and individual behaviours. In a world where the marketplace and the media dictate morality and ethics, it is little wonder that juvenilization is so pervasive and forceful. As an aside, it is ironic to contemplate that all this came about through the inadvertent efforts of those espousing puritanical morality and ethics – the very antithesis of our contemporary Epicureanism. The Industrial Revolution was fostered and controlled initially by Oliver Cromwell's Puritan descendants, who associated the accumulation of goods with the gaining of spiritual favour. Shortly thereafter, with the spread of the market economy and the need to generate profits through increased consumption, it was the advertiser who took over the role of the preacher, proclaiming an autonomous consumerist faith and the means of attaining paradise on earth through consumption.

Juvenilization surfaced, first, in the domain of music. In the 1920s, jazz music – once strictly the domain of the brothels in Kansas City and New Orleans – started to flourish across the United States as the musical idiom of young and sexually attractive people, who tuned *en masse* into the music of jazz bandleaders on their radios. In 1923, the Broadway musical *Running Wild* helped turn the Charleston into a dance craze for the young – a dance that brought out into the open the carefree sexuality of adolescence. There was, of course, a reaction against such trends from society's elders. Prohibition and a general censure of such musical trends were two outcomes of this reaction. But juvenilization had started in full earnest and could not be curtailed. It was then, and is now, a two-edged sword. While it challenged the stodgy, puritanical status quo, it also induced people to believe that their youth was the only valuable thing to hold on to for life – especially in the realms of musical taste, fashion, and language (as I will argue in subsequent chapters).

By the late 1920s, the cheapness and availability of mass-produced records led to a true shift in cultural aesthetics – the entrenchment of pop music as mainstream music. Despite pop's apparent lack of 'classical good taste,' people have always loved it, no matter how controversial or crass it may appear to music purists. For instance, the Glenn Miller style of music – which became not only a new kind of dance music but also a youth lifestyle 'code' – still stimulates and excites us to dance and enjoy ourselves. Miller hits such as 'Little Brown Jug,' 'Sunrise Serenade,' 'Moonlight Serenade,' and 'In the Mood' are still played and enjoyed widely to this day by individuals of all age groups. Miller disbanded his orchestra in 1942 and enlisted in the U.S. Army, where he formed the forty-two-piece, all-star Army Air Force Band, which entertained Second World War service personnel with regular radio broadcasts. In 1944, Miller died when his small plane, headed to Paris, disappeared over the English Channel during bad weather. He thus became one of the first 'mythical heroes' of contemporary pop culture. His influence on the spread of this culture is unmistakable. In the years subsequent to the war, Miller-style 'swing' became a society-wide phenomenon.

Shortly thereafter, singing idol Frank Sinatra, who started out as a 'swinger' wowing the bobby-soxer teens of the late 1940s in New York, gave America a foretaste of the hysteria that rock music would generate in the subsequent decade. In the same time frame, a 'generation gap' emerged, pitting adolescents against their parents, leading to the publication of such unprecedented guidebooks for parents as *How to Live with Your Teenager* (1953) and *Understanding Teenagers* (1955). Magazines directed specifically at teenagers (*Dig, Teen, Teen World, Sixteen, Teen Romances*, etc.) – telling them how to become attractive and to interact with parents – became popular at the same time, further entrenching the gap. They replaced, *tout court*, the advice that parents themselves were once expected to give their adolescents. Such advice was increasingly characterized as 'old-fashioned' and 'out of date.' The term *cool* became a shibboleth. 'Being cool' meant hanging out with peers, going to parties, smoking cigarettes, consuming alcohol, engaging casually in sexual activities, and making one's physical appearance different from that of adults (by means of cosmetics, hairstyle, dress, etc.).

The gap between the generations was captured superbly in fiction by the American novelist J.D. Salinger (1919–) in his masterpiece, *The Catcher in the Rye*. The main character of the novel, Holden Caulfield, remains to this day a symbol of the troubled, troublesome, and insubordinate teenager. The book came out in 1951, but various portions of it were published as far back as 1945 in *Collier's* and *The New Yorker*. In a sanitarium, the sixteen-year-old Holden, who has been suspended from his preparatory school, retells the events of the previous few days to a psychiatrist, just before he suffers a nervous breakdown during Christmas vacation. Disgusted by the hypocrisy of adult society, Holden is especially repelled by the social masks that he perceives adults to wear and by their dreary habits. He desperately hopes to protect his younger sister, Phoebe, from growing up and losing her innocence and purity. The novel also paints memorable portraits of adolescent personalities. Robert Ackley, one of Holden's dorm mates at school, for instance, would be called a 'loser' or 'grosser' today, because of his disgusting habits and his physical and social awkwardness. Holden's roommate, Ward Stradlater, on the other hand, is the first fictional 'cool guy,' a superficial character whose only preoccupation in life is 'looking cool.' It was such idiotic lifestyles that drove Holden to the brink.

Salinger's portrait of adolescence was uncannily prophetic. By the mid-1950s, a whole generation of Ackleys and Stradlaters came to have their own music, 'rock and roll' – a euphemism for sexual intercourse, connoting the throbbing rhythms connected with incipient sexual feelings put artificially on hold by social strictures. Through recordings, radio exposure, television shows, and movies, rock musicians were turned into overnight idols. Rock stars influenced clothing and hairstyle fashions and spread dance crazes. Adolescents turned to pop-music lyrics for advice on what to do and for insight into their romantic experiences, largely ignoring what their parents said. By the end of the decade, it was clear that musicians and the media had taken over the role of 'village elders.'

The 1950s also witnessed the emergence of bizarre new coming-of-age rites that the adolescents themselves institutionalized through the media. As mentioned above, traditional cultures have always marked the passage from childhood to adulthood in specific ritualistic ways.

City societies largely abandoned such rituals centuries ago. But the need for them has not disappeared. What occurred in the market-driven and media-shaped adolescent culture of the 1950s bears witness to this very fact. The 'sixteenth birthday party' became an ersatz passage rite created by the teenagers themselves in partnership with the media – I mention, as cases in point, titles of songs such as 'Sixteen Candles' and 'Happy Birthday, Sweet Sixteen,' which hit the top of the charts. The locus for the enactment of the rite was the high school prom. It became clear that the high school had become the adolescent's distinctive social universe – a place where friendship covenants and courtship rituals went hand in hand with academic interests. As Lynd and Lynd had already observed in the late 1920s, 'The high school, with its athletics, clubs, sororities and fraternities, dances and parties, and other extracurricular activities is a fairly complete social cosmos in itself, and about this city within a city the social life of the intermediate generation centers.'[13] No wonder that friendships forged in high school today tend to be permanent, whereas those contracted earlier or later in life tend to be perfunctory and transitory.

By the 1960s, the marriage between adolescence and the media-based pop culture was completely consummated. Rock music came to play a larger and larger role in the lifestyles of teens. In the 1950s, there was *one* hit parade for everyone. By the start of the 1960s, there were several hit parades, reflecting a growing diversity in youth lifestyles. As rapid change became the mode and the mood, a new symptomatology emerged, aptly called *neomania* by the French social critic Roland Barthes.[14] Barthes defined neomania as a constant craving for new objects of consumption and new forms of entertainment induced by the media.

By the middle part of the decade, something unexpected happened, much to the chagrin of the business world. The teenagers themselves became aware that they were pawns of the media. They started questioning the values that a consumerist and media-driven society espoused. The new 'Holden Caulfields' started, in effect, to reject the very culture that had spawned and institutionalized adolescence. They denounced the 'adult establishment' as the cause of the world's political and social ills. They even turned away from the aesthetic traditions of the West, seeking inspiration from Eastern traditions to fashion a new rock and roll, which spearheaded their clamour for social change. The rock concert became a 'happening' of great political and ideological proportions, spurring on youths to social activism. Drugs were consumed at such concerts to induce or heighten the aesthetic experience of the whole event. Sexual intercourse was practised openly, in obvious defiance of adult moralism. In a bizarre way, what Plato (c. 427–347 B.C.) feared about music millennia ago had come about in the 'counter-culture' world of the 1960s. As he aptly put it: 'For the introduction of a new kind of music must be shunned as imperiling the whole state; since styles of music are never disturbed without affecting the most important political institutions.'[15] Counter-culture rock was, at first, subversive in the Platonic sense. The Beatles then raised it to new levels of artistic expression in their album *Sgt. Pepper's Lonely Hearts Club Band* (1967). By the end of the decade, rock operas such as *Tommy* (1969), by the Who, were being considered as serious musical works by mainstream music critics.

But, alas, the counter-culture mood did not last long; it waned by the mid-1970s. The revolutionaries had, simply, become older and less inclined to revolt, as they started to have children of their own. Ironically, as their own children grew into adolescence, the ex-revolutionary parents became terrified. Because of the explicit sexual and satanic themes they appeared to glorify, the recordings of some of the new bands came under the scrutiny of new censorship-minded groups. Plato's warning was reverberating in the minds of the ex-hippies themselves. But their fears were unfounded. Indeed, the juvenilization process at work in society at large ensured that such trends would quickly pass, with ever-new trends just around the corner.

One particular trend really scared the heck out of the parents of the era – given its genuine subversive intent. It was called 'punk rock.' Those who called themselves 'punks' at first were British and American teens who came from the working class. Feeling alienated from mainstream culture, they genuinely threatened the social order by inveighing violently against it through their messages and actions. They were anti-bourgeois and anti-capitalist in ways that the counter-culture revolutionaries of the previous teen generation themselves found shocking and offensive. Punk concerts were deliberately violent and confrontational. Members of punk rock bands spat on their audiences, mutilated themselves with knives, damaged the props on stage and in the hall, and incited their audiences to do the same. The fashion trends they introduced for their followers – chains, dog collars, black clothes, army boots, shaved heads and wild-looking 'Mohawk' hairdos of every colour imaginable – were menacing and degrading at the same time. Their music was the rock equivalent of Andy Warhol's sculptures or of John Cage's compositions – it was sardonic, absurdist, preposterous, aleatory, and 'do it yourself.' Musicians played random notes, banged their guitars, shouted, burped, urinated, and bellowed at will on stage to a basic rhythmic pulsating beat.

But, as it turned out, punk also passed on as a mere trend, as punk songs, fashions, and even language were co-opted by the media and recycled into society at large, where they lost their abrasiveness and shock effect, becoming nothing more than alternative lifestyle trends. Other bizarre trends suffered the same fate. *The Rocky Horror Picture Show,* for instance, was at first a truly worrisome craze. The movie became a cult phenomenon, with hordes of adolescents going to see it week after week, month after month, year after year. It was both a parody of the inanity of 1950s rock and a coded performance ritual extolling a new type of weird sexual lifestyle. As Greenwald remarks, it was both an attempt 'to shock by departing from the tradition of rock and roll machismo established by Elvis,' and a new 'grammar of cool' that favoured 'makeup, cross dressing, and an overall smearing of the lines between the generations and the sexes.'[16] The cult movie had staying power; but it, too, did not last. However, it made the blurring of gender roles the subtext of the music styles and stage performances of many other pop stars and bands, such as the hard rock band Kiss, whose performances on stage were a transvestite, transgender, and transmedia 'put-on.' Each member of the band adopted a comic-book persona and wore a special type of *pagliaccio* makeup. Their circus-type stage act included fireworks and the smashing of their own instruments.

Running in opposition to such 'shock-schlock' trends was 'disco' culture, epitomized in the 1978 movie *Saturday Night Fever,* starring John Travolta. Disco was a throwback to the days of swing and ballroom dancing. The disco scene attracted hordes of teens – all apparently afflicted by the same type of Saturday night fever as their hero, Travolta. But a few years after the movie, disco faded. By the mid-1980s, a new rebellious mood crystallized. It found its musical voice in 'rap' and 'hip-hop.' But, as shall be discussed in the fourth chapter, that mood, too, did not last very long, even though, as I write, it still holds a wide appeal among young people. By the late 1990s, in fact, the 'subversive overtones' of rap and hip-hop had become part of a new media code designed simply to entertain rather than defy.

The rapid turnover in music trends and their associated lifestyle codes is the only constant in our 'forever young' world. The current economic system will survive, arguably, only by ensuring that constant change is, indeed, the only constant. No wonder, then, that the media are saturated with images of youth. In the late 1990s, tweenie females could be seen putting on belly shirts, frosted lipstick, wobbly footwear, and blue nail polish in imitation of such 'girl stars' as Britney Spears and the Spice Girls – to mention some of the more widely known ones at the time. Tweenie males wore baggy pants and earrings in imitation of rapper and hip-hop musicians; or else they 'spiked' their hair in imitation of certain male cinema models and rock stars. Significantly, these became items in a general fashion code – worn by tweenies, adolescents, and adults alike. To this day, one can walk into any clothing store and see virtually no difference between the clothing fashions intended for tweenies, teenagers, or adults. A mother could wear her ten-year-old daughter's clothes without getting a second look, and the daughter could wear her mother's clothes without appearing in any way precocious.

By ensuring that teenage lifestyle patterns are redirected to the social mainstream, we have, in effect, created the illusion that the fountain of youth is available for anyone of any age to drink from. But this illusion has led to a truly 'unhealthy' situation, culturally. It has, in effect, eliminated the 'wise elder' from the social radar screen. That is why people turn to the media, or psychologists and social workers, or self-help books for advice, rather than to older people such as grandparents. But these 'experts' are hardly capable replacements for 'the elders.' We have mistaken material well-being for spiritual well-being. And the latter cannot be denied, as I argue throughout this book. The fountain of youth has, it would seem, become filled to the brim with contaminated water. And the time has come to question why we continue to drink from it.

The image of a seventy-year-old Deadhead swaying her hips in synch with a thirteen-year-old Deadhead is a disconcerting one in many ways. Maybe bridging the generation gap can only be done in such a way today; but then again, maybe not. That pleasant-looking lady was a 'teenager of yesterday.' And, in some way or other, virtually any adult alive today could easily exchange places with her, with no one making anything of it. But dressing and looking like adolescents is hardly a meaningful way of communicating with them. Adolescents do, indeed, need to communicate with adults, but in a way that is more meaningful, *more mature*. I remember my own grandfather providing me with great insights into my adolescent life experiences by simply discussing some proverb or wise saying with me. Adolescents need their grandfathers and grandmothers to be wise and judicious, whether or not they listen to, and still groove to, the music of the Grateful Dead.

Many blame juvenilization on the generation known as the 'baby boomers.' Between the years 1946 and 1964, a baby boom of unprecedented magnitude took place in North America. During that period, 77 million babies were born. Already in 1957, the new boomer youth market was worth more than $30 billion a year. The boomers were, in effect, the first true 'rockers.' And for their extravagant lifestyles they have been the targets of acerbic criticism.[17] As Douglas Owram observes, the boomers have become society's pariahs, because of their ambivalence. They spawned the counter-culture revolution and the civil rights and women's movements; indeed, if gender and race discrimination have taken a beating in the last few decades, it is because of the valiant efforts of the boomers. But they were also behind the popularity of such frivolous things as Barbie dolls and T-shirts.[18] And what really annoys subsequent generations about them is the fact that they continue to see themselves as 'hip,' even more 'than their own kids,' as social critic Bruce Pollock puts it.[19] The reverence for Elvis Presley, for instance, that a large segment of the boomer generation continues to have is truly perverse. Presley died on 16 August 1977. Since then, there have been constant pilgrimages to his house; his records and movies are being continually reissued; and many fans even keep shrines to his memory and tokens from his life (vials of his sweat, scraps of carpet from his house, etc.) in their homes. Recently, Elvis was immortalized on a U.S. stamp. Elvis's music was, and continues to be, fun. The fact that it has become the stuff of legend is the legacy of the boomers – so the critics tell us.

The harshest portrayal of the boomer generation has come, ironically, from the institutions that have catered constantly to boomer tastes – the media. TV sitcoms in the 1980s and 1990s that parodied and satirized the boomers were the norm. Take, as a case in point, *Married ... with Children*. The father on that program, Al Bundy, was caricatured as a reprehensible boomer with a family just as shallow and despicable as he was. Bundy was the opposite of the wise and judicious TV dads of the 1950s, such as Jim Anderson of *Father Knows Best*. Bundy simply had never grown up, but instead constantly yearned for his own particular brand of 1950s teenage lifestyle. He was a downtrodden, inept, vulgar boor who had all the wrong answers to family problems and who always felt sorry for himself. His boomer wife, Peggy, sported a moronic hairdo and was constantly struggling to make Al more sexually interested in her. His children, Bud and Kelly, were similarly caricatured as boorish, rude, and sex-crazed. There was no sugar-coating in that sitcom. It was a cynical parody of the boomer generation.

But are such media portrayals of the boomers correct? Or are the boomers convenient scapegoats? They were, after all, the first generation of teenagers courted specifically by the media, because of the amount of leisure time they had at their disposal and their propensity to consume and spend. I can give no answers to such questions. However, one thing is for certain: the role of the boomers in the development of the modern world cannot be assessed in isolation from the larger process that I have called juvenilization. And that process started long before the boomers were born.

In my view, the ambivalent image that we have developed of the boomers is an outcome of media representations. In the 1950s, TV programs such as *Father Knows Best*, *The Honeymooners*, and *The Adventures of Ozzie and Harriet* sculpted the father figure to fit the requirements of the traditional patriarchal family. Most of the early sitcoms painted the family in a rosy light. Jim Anderson, in *Father Knows Best*, was in charge, with his wife working behind the scenes to maintain harmony through subservience. That portrayal of family life not only reflected the social mind-set of the 1950s with regard to the family, it probably generated it. In reality, there was great diversity in family life in that decade – a diversity that television itself captured somewhat in sitcoms such as *The Honeymooners* and *I Love Lucy*, both of which revolved around strong-willed wives who were, in effect, precursors of later feminist characters on television.

In the 1960s and early 1970s, the TV subtext changed as Jim Anderson's boomer children grew up and joined the counter-culture revolution. The boomers were in the spotlight for the first time. The sitcom that reflected the new generation gap (between boomers and their parents) was *All in the Family*. The North American continent was divided, ideologically and emotionally, into two camps – those who supported the views and attitudes of the TV father, Archie Bunker, a staunch defender of the Vietnam War, and those who despised the war and thus the persona of Archie Bunker. What was happening inside the TV Bunker family was apparently happening in families across the continent. North American society had entered a period of emotional turmoil and bitter debate over such controversial issues as the war, racism, the role of women in society, and the hegemony of the patriarchal family.

The total 'deconstruction' of the 1950s family became apparent in many of the 1980s and 1990s sitcoms. One of these – *The Simpsons* – was an ingenious cartoon parody that became a huge success, debuting in 1987 and, as I write, still popular. Homer Simpson, the father on the program, is the boomer anti-hero, who, like Al Bundy, has all the wrong answers to family problems. He is rude and stupid. But the program is, overall, interesting. It has even become a target of academic discussion. In an interesting collection of studies, *The Simpsons and Philosophy* (2001), edited by Irwin, Conrad, and Skoble, the claim is made that the program deals on a regular basis with some of the greatest questions of philosophy and religion.[20] I remain unconvinced that a sitcom has the capacity to do anything of the kind in any meaningful way. It is akin to playing, say, a Beethoven symphony on a kazoo. The melody is the same, but its delivery has a buzzing and quacking quality to it, thus demeaning it considerably. Analogously, I find it bizarre that the same kind of profundity that is ascribed to the discourse utilized by a Plato, an Aristotle, or a Nietzsche could also be ascribed to the discourse utilized by a cartoon character such as Homer Simpson. Only in a media-driven pop-culture world is such a thing possible.

In the early part of the twenty-first century, television provided a host of new 'father figures' for the consumption of increasingly diverse audiences. Some new prime-time dads were throwbacks to Jim Anderson and Bill Cosby. I mention, as cases in point, the Reverend Eric Camden of *7th Heaven* and veterinarian Jim Hansen of *Providence*, who may already have disappeared from the medium as this book goes to print. Other dads, however, continue to be brutally parodied, in the tradition of sitcoms such as *The Simpsons*. There is little doubt that television will continue to recycle father figures, mother figures, and the like, constantly; it will change the details of such figures, not their substance.

The Forever Young Syndrome

Images of youth are everywhere. Magazines are replete with photographs of Adonises and Aphrodites – in Greek mythology, Adonis was the handsome youth loved by Aphrodite, the goddess of love and beauty. The women are slim, sexy, and fashionably tough looking. The men are muscular, slim, and self-absorbed. *MH-18*, a male teen magazine that started publishing in the late 1990s, contains advice to boys and young men on how to bleach or dye their hair and on what kinds of cologne and jewellery to wear in certain situations – mirroring a concern about body image that, once, was considered to be a female phenomenon among teenagers. The popularity of 'boy bands' such as 'N Sync, 98 Degrees, and Backstreet Boys, as well as of Latino artists such as Ricky Martin and Julio Iglesias, Jr, made it acceptable for male teens to worry openly about their looks. As I write, this obsession with looks continues unabated.

Such trends are part of a symptomatology that has been generated by what can be called a widespread 'forever young syndrome' (FYS). The effects of this syndrome on individuals are hard to identify and examine objectively, because they are so diffuse and variable. One concrete effect is an unprecedented increase in the sales of cosmetics and in the use of plastic surgery by males and females of all ages and all social classes. In the not-too-distant past, the 'facial rejuvenation business' was primarily for Hollywood actors and actresses in their sixties. The American Society of Plastic Surgeons reported in 2002 that nearly 2 million people, many of them in their forties and fifties, underwent some kind of facial rejuvenation procedure in 2001. Another visible effect is the widespread tendency of more and more adults to maintain their previous adolescent lifestyles throughout their lives, albeit unconsciously. People hold onto the music of their teen years and continue worshipping the media idols of their youth well into middle age (and even old age). A third effect is the general tendency for individuals of all ages to adopt, in some form, the fashions and lifestyles that emanate from the adolescent realm.

Needless to say, not everyone in our culture is afflicted by the FYS. There are many who, as a matter of fact, react vehemently against the silly juvenile trends that spread quickly to society at large. But it is also true that many, if not most, now take little notice of such trends. The source of the FYS is the media 'distraction factory,' as the social critic Goodwin has designated it.[21] But therein lies the rub – as Shakespeare aptly put it. The factory is both good and bad. It produces trivial works such as the *Scream* movies and artistically acclaimed movies such as *Amadeus* and *One Flew over the Cuckoo's Nest*. In this factory, charlatans and artists are strangely intertwined. The inanity of a Limp Bizkit or an Eminem is put next to the magnificence of a Philip Glass or a Nino Rota. The media oligarchy has replaced the aristocracy and the church as a sponsor of the arts – but it is a Janus-faced sponsor. In Roman mythology, Janus was the god of gates and doorways, depicted with two faces looking in opposite directions. Today, the media have become the gods of the 'gates and doorways of aesthetics,' looking in opposite directions – one pointing towards distraction and the other towards engagement.

The distraction factory was erected in the mid-1920s. That was the era when radio became, along with film, a highly popular mass medium, shaping trends in music, programming, advertising, and verbal communication generally. Radio could reach many more people than print, not only because it could span great distances instantly but also because its audiences did not necessarily have to be print literate. Programming could thus be designed with mass appeal. As a consequence, radio spawned pop culture – a culture for all, not just for the literati and the *cognoscenti*.

The distraction factory was expanded with the advent of television. The first television sets for mass utilization became available in England in 1936 and in the United States in 1938. After the Second World War, technical improvements and prosperity led to a growing demand for these sets. In the United States, six television stations were established at first, each one broadcasting for only a few hours each day. By 1948, thirty-four all-day stations were in operation in twenty-one major cities, and about one million television sets had been sold. By the end of the 1950s, national television networks were established in most industrialized countries. Television had emerged, in effect, to replace radio as the primary source of mass distraction virtually across the world. As the twentieth century came to a close, television entered the computer age with the advent of digital and web TV – television transmitted in a digital format and accessible through the Internet.

With the widespread growth of cable television and then of Direct-Broadcast-Satellite services in the 1990s, many new channels and types of programming became available to people across the globe. As a consequence, debates about television's impact on children, world culture, politics, and community life have since become common and widespread. On the one side, critics say that television feeds a constant stream of simplified ideas and sensationalistic images to unwitting viewers, that it negatively influences politics and voting patterns, that it destroys local cultures in favour of a bland, Hollywood-based distraction culture, and that it encourages passivity in people. On the other side, defenders say that television provides a great deal of high-quality educational and cultural programming and that it is the major source of local, national, and international news for many citizens who would otherwise remain uninformed. Whatever the truth, one thing is for certain – television has turned out to be *the* technological invention that has consolidated what the great Canadian communications theorist Marshall McLuhan (1911–80) called the global village, because it has made the same pattern and kind of distraction (the same TV sitcoms, adventure programs, music, and variety shows) available across the globe.

And there is little doubt that in this village one general outlook prevails – the tendency of its inhabitants to think of themselves as 'forever young' and attractive, both physically and socially, just like the actors and personalities they see day in and day out on television, in advertisements, and in movies. Media innovation takes its cue from the young, who are thus always in the avant-garde of trends. Already in 1952, the American author and columnist Max Lerner (1902–) wrote in the *New York Post* (4 June) that 'Having a thirteen-year-old in the family is like having a general-admission ticket to the movies, radio and TV, because you get to understand that the glittering new arts of our civilization are directed to the teen-agers, and by their suffrage they stand or fall.' Decades later, things have not changed one iota. Virtually the entire media–entertainment industry today depends for its economic survival on capturing the 'teen dollar.' For this reason, it caters primarily to the adolescent market. There is a veritable synergy today between that industry and adolescent lifestyles – they influence each other in tandem.

This implicit pact between the media and teens was forged, as discussed above, in the 1950s. Before that, it was difficult to find a movie or novel that dealt with adolescence, or that even involved adolescents as actors or characters. Today, by contrast, it is difficult to find a movie or a television program that does not deal with some adolescent theme or involve adolescents as actors.

How did this come about? By the time of the counter-culture movement of the 1960s, it was a matter of survival for business to embrace outright the new images of youth insurgency, and thus to 'change with the times.' One highly effective early strategy of this 'if-you-can't-beat-them-join-them' approach was the development of an advertising style that mocked consumerism and advertising itself! The strategy worked beyond expectations. As social critic Frank Thomas has skilfully argued,[22] being young and rebellious came to mean having a 'cool look'; being anti-establishment and subversive entailed wearing 'hip clothes.' 'New' and 'different' became the shibboleths of the advertising and marketing lexicon, coaxing people into buying goods not because they really needed them but simply because they were 'new,' 'cool,' 'hip.'

Campaigns, such as those of the 'Pepsi Generation' and the Coke universal brotherhood, directly incorporated the rhetoric and symbolism of the hippie counter-culture, thus creating the illusion that the goals of the hippies and of the soft-drink manufacturers were one and the same. Rebellion through purchasing became the subliminal thread woven into advertising subtexts by ingenious marketing strategists. The 'Dodge Rebellion' and 'Oldsmobile Youngmobile' campaigns followed the soft-drink campaigns, etching into the nomenclature of products themselves the powerful connotations of hippie rebellion and defiance. Even a sewing company, alas, came forward to urge people to join its own type of surrogate revolution with its slogan 'You don't let the establishment make your world; don't let it make your clothes.' In effect, by claiming to 'join the revolution,' advertising created the real revolution. That is why, since the late 1960s, the worlds of advertising, marketing, and entertainment have become totally intertwined with youth lifestyle movements, both responding and contributing to rapid fluctuations in social trends and values. An implicit 'trust' between the media and the young thus was forged, proposing marketplace solutions to social problems. The business world had discovered fortuitously in the counter-culture era how to incorporate the powerful images of youth protest into the 'grammar' of everyday life. The only authentic rebel of the counter-culture was, according to many, Abbie Hoffman, whose *Steal This Book* – a handbook of how to survive by stealing that Hoffman wanted readers to shoplift from stores – was the only kind of subversive gesture that was perceived as truly hostile and menacing to the corporate world order. The other revolutionaries were, in hindsight, really adolescents doing no more than waging battles with their parents and with one another.

Today, one hardly notices that trends in the adolescent world are recycled and marketed as the fashion styles of all shortly after their invention.[23] Rock music is no longer limited to an audience of teenagers, since many current listeners formed their musical tastes growing up to some previous style of rock and roll. All this is not only good for business, it is indispensable to it. In its 9 August 2000 issue, the *Wall Street Journal* pointed out that there are more teens today than ever before, because in each of the years from 1989 to 1993, births in the United States exceeded 4 million for the first time since the early 1960s. Teens now spend more than $150 billion annually, making them one of the most important market segments around. Not surprisingly, a cottage industry of consultants, ad executives, and marketing researchers has sprung up to help corporations gain access to the increasingly lucrative, yet highly unstable, teen market. That is why new gadgets of technology are directed at teens. It is little wonder that teens, attracted by the images of cool that technological advertising promotes, are often the household's 'experts' when it comes to new digital products and thus the ones who influence what parents will buy. They trek to school with cellphones, pagers, and Palm Pilots – all of which, incidentally, promise to become themselves advertising vehicles. In recent interviews with teens, I have found that the Internet is much more stimulating to them than television. One teen put it this way: 'I spend my time mainly playing games on-line, and checking out sites or communicating with friends on-line; maybe four hours a day. TV is boring, man, you just sit there; at least here I entertain myself any way I want to.' A computer has, in fact, become a radio, a television, a movie theatre, a library, a magazine, and a newspaper all in one. The cellphone and the on-line form of communication are fast replacing all other forms. Soon, kids will know how to design a Web page before they can spell. Even television is becoming increasingly sensitive to the new 'digital teens.' Networks and specialty-channel programs are constantly emitting blurbs inviting viewers to visit them on-line. All this will dictate the future course of adolescence and, perhaps, even transform it radically. If teens will indeed be going on-line *en masse*, then cliquing and hanging out will become less fashionable, as the 'virtual clique' might replace the real one. Whatever happens, one thing is for certain – developments in technology and developments in adolescence are now totally intertwined.

This phenomenon applies especially to change in language. Through electronic chat rooms, teens have started abbreviating language and putting their imprint indelibly on it. In a recent study of Internet language, which he labels Netspeak, the linguist David Crystal notes that spelling has become simplified so that a message can be sent in the shortest time possible.[24] Hence, sentences showing abbreviations and simplified spelling patterns such as the following now abound in English.[25]

- *brb* (I'll be right back)
- *g2g* (I have got to go)
- *hhok* (Ha ha; I'm only kidding)
- *how ya doin* (How are you doing?)
- *i dont know why* (I don't know why)
- *i fine* (I am fine)
- *i got enuf* (I've got enough)
- *imho* (In my humble opinion)
- *it wuz lotsa fun* (It was lots of fun)
- *tttt* (To tell the truth)
- *u feeling better now?* (Are you feeling better now?)
- *wanna know why* (Do you want to know why?)
- *you da right person* (You're the right person)

Young people are in the vanguard of the processes that now under-gird linguistic change as they exploit the possibilities of digital technology, radically changing the face of literacy. Media programming, too, has become thoroughly linked with adolescence. TV comedy, for instance, is frequently moronic in its use of adolescent humour. Some programs can only be deciphered by teens. In the mid-1990s, *Beavis and Butthead*, for example, was designed to appeal primarily to male teens. It was one of MTV's top-rated shows, hated by parents, loved by teens. Beavis had reddish-brown hair, Butthead brown hair and braces. The two characters sat together at the back of a high school classroom, picking their noses. Typical verbal exchanges between them included: 'Cool,' 'Sucks' (school sucks, life sucks), 'Nachos rule,' 'Burn it,' 'Dude,' 'Chicks,' 'Ass,' 'Asswipe.' They spent a lot of their time watching music videos and TV commercials. In a phrase, they were adolescent boors. But they were a hit, as is the 2002 DVD *Beavis: The History of Beavis and Butthead*, recalling and legitimizing their programs as central chapters in the history of contemporary pop culture. Capitalizing on the success of *Beavis and Butthead*, the TV moguls came up with a female counterpart in 1997, *Daria Morgendorffer*. The eponymous heroine was an expressionless high schooler with black glasses, dispensing wry witticisms *à la* Beavis and Butthead. Incredibly, her 'dorky look' was adopted as a cool new look by many females in society at large during that era.

The promulgation of 'disgusting' teen humour is not restricted to such teen-directed programs. It is noticeable everywhere. Take, for instance, *South Park*, a popular program that began in the 1990s and is still going strong as I write. This sitcom can perhaps be characterized as a 'comedy of vulgarity,' parodying digestion, defecation, flatulence, and copulation. It is a kind of *Beavis and Butthead* program gone amok. Although the satirical thrust of the program is rather transparent, its vulgar style makes it little more than an outlet for post-adolescent humour. The general principle guiding its form of satire can be expressed as 'the more vulgar and disgusting, the funnier.' There have, of course, been adult programs of this type, such as the British *Monty Python* shows. But those never degenerated into the type of vulgar buffoonery that can be fully appreciated only by a particular age group. Many of the ancient satirists, too, delighted in putting vulgarity on display on the stage. But in all cases, the displayers were adult, and the mode of humour was in line with a certain literary tradition.

In a way, *South Park* is preferable to the many current soppy sitcoms and adult crime, lawyer, and adventure shows, where self-centred characters are wrapped up in their wearisome personal problems. At least *South Park* is not sanctimonious. Its subtext is, essentially, 'Laugh at life and at the stupidity of it all.' Through caricature and hackneyed images, reality is held up for derision; and social stereotypes and people who buy into them are ridiculed constantly. The audience, not the subject matter, is the butt of the jokes. Nevertheless, the program is juvenile. It gets airtime because it is disgusting and sophomoric. Its type of humour has invaded mass culture. Blatant or suggested flatulence, for example, has been used in such mainstream movies as *The Mighty Ducks*, *The Lion King*, and *Little Giants*, all made for young audiences. Irreverent logos and expressions now appear regularly on T-shirts and caps – 'Snot Candy,' 'Gummy Boogers,' 'Monster Warts,' and so on. Wholesomeness simply does not sell in a market that is driven by juvenilized tastes.

But how realistic are such media portrayals of teens? In my interviews, I found a fairly widespread critique of such trends on the part of adolescents themselves. Moreover, the media have forgotten that teens can find as much if not more delight and inspiration in 'adult art' as adults can. The great works of music, art, and literature have as much of a transformative effect on adolescents today as they have had on people of all ages in the past. Parenthetically, it would seem that these have an overall beneficial effect on people of all ages. There are solid data to suggest that even minimal exposure to the music of Mozart, for instance, benefits both children and adults in many ways.[26]

The image-makers of our culture would have us believe that we can find the magical fountain of youth by indulging in the accoutrements of youth and by adopting youth lifestyles. But, like the Spanish explorer Juan Ponce de Léon (1460–1521), who searched for the magical fountain he had heard of from the Native Americans, we are in danger of going astray and ending up in a sorry situation. In 1512, Ponce obtained permission from the Spanish king to find, conquer, and colonize Bimini (where the fountain was purportedly located). On 27 March he sighted the eastern shore of the present state of Florida, which he believed to be the legendary Bimini. He named the region *Florida* because he sighted it on Easter Sunday (Spanish, *Pascua florida*: 'flowery Easter'). Ponce not only never found the fountain, but he ended up dead in battle at the age of fifty for his efforts.

It has become abundantly clear to me that unmasking the cultural sources of the modern-day version of Ponce's delusional search for the fountain of youth is critical for understanding who we are and where we should be going from here. That is the objective of the remaining chapters.

CHAPTER TWO

Looking like Teenagers

The pursuit of beauty is much more dangerous nonsense than the pursuit of truth or goodness, because it affords a stronger temptation to the ego.

Northrop Frye (1912–1991)

The Greek myth of Narcissus holds a special warning today for those of us who live in a forever young society. It can be paraphrased as follows. One day in the woods, the nymph Echo met a handsome youth with whom she fell deeply in love. Echo stretched out her arms imploringly to him. But the conceited youth cruelly rebuffed her amorous gesture. Humiliated, Echo went to hide in a cave, where she wasted away until nothing was left of her but her voice. The goddess Nemesis witnessed the youth's heartless act of shunning and, to punish him, made him fall in love with his own face as he saw it reflected in a pool. Unable to remove himself from his image, the youth gradually withered away, changing into the narcissus plant.

Having the financial capability and leisure time to spoil and pamper oneself with the latest fashions and cosmetics was once the exclusive privilege of aristocrats – who (as a consequence) were considered to be too self-indulgent and narcissistic to be able to withstand any hardships that life presented to them. Now, self-indulgence and narcissism are the privilege of virtually everyone. Today's collective narcissism impels common folk to sculpt and maintain an ageless look. It is a phenomenon that goes largely unnoticed. The wearer of a particular clothing style, in fact, could be eight or fifty-eight and no one would make anything of it. But the warning built into the myth of Narcissus cannot be ignored – we risk falling in love with our own image to the detriment of everything else. In traditional cultures, separate dress and grooming codes for males and females, young and old, aristocrats and peasants were always (and continue to be) strictly enforced to signal critical differences in social role, age, and status. In modern societies, many of these distinctions have disappeared. But their disappearance is hardly the result of some well-meaning democratic movement. Rather, it is, arguably, the outcome of an obsessive narcissism that has been engendered by affluence. And this has had consequences for virtually everyone. Today, even those who cannot really afford to 'look the look' will often go deeply into debt in order to keep up with the fashions perpetrated by the images of young Narcissuses (male and female) in movies, TV programs, and advertisements. Virtually no one wants to dress 'like an old person.' In fact, the latter phrase has virtually no meaning any longer.

Looking fashionably young has become an implicit norm, and only frail health or economic destitution seem to keep people from striving to do so. In this chapter, I therefore start my search for the sources of the FYS (forever young syndrome) in a critical domain – the domain of 'image.'

Body Image

Needless to say, not everyone in our culture aspires to carve out and maintain a fashionable, up-to-date appearance. Many people, young and old alike, are aware of, and horrified by, the ravages to the psyche brought about by our media-driven narcissism. But it is true to say that 'looking the look' is now part of a largely unconscious groupthink. That is why no one makes anything of a seventy-year-old person wearing a Grateful Dead T-shirt – as I mentioned in the previous chapter. The danger of our modern-day narcissism is, in fact, that it is not easily detectable as such. It resides practically unnoticed as a hidden pattern in our groupthink. And, as I will argue in this chapter, it is a primary symptom of the FYS.

To articulate my argument, I will refer to three modalities of 'maturity' – the physical, the social, and the personal. *Physical maturity* is a process of nature. It occurs at puberty, and its manifestations are, logically, *physical*. Shortly after the advent of puberty, the human body starts showing the ineluctable and irreversible signs of aging. These vary considerably in the time when they first appear and in the severity of their occurrence from one individual to another. But old we will all become, sooner or later – a statement that, as self-evident as it is, needs expression today. *Social maturity* – assuming the responsibilities of adulthood – is a matter of convention. Traditional cultures expect social maturity to coincide with physical maturity. And, needless to say, wherever this expectation exists today, the two maturational modalities do indeed coincide. In our own culture, by contrast, a pubescent individual is seen as lacking in social maturity, as needing more time to grow up and mature further. That is why we continue to view adolescents as basically children. If there is an imbalance between physical and social maturation today, it is because we expect there to be one. *Individual maturity* is the individual's particular mode of adaptation to society's maturation conventions. It, too, is off balance in our culture. Indeed, it is not unusual to encounter fifteen-year-olds who are more 'mature' than some fifty-year-olds who cling desperately to their youth – the so-called Elvii (those who continue to revere Elvis Presley) and Deaners (those who continue to revere James Dean) are cases in point.

The repercussions of such imbalances are evident everywhere. One of these is the perilous view of body image that many adolescents develop during the process of physical maturation. The term *body image* can be defined simply as a perception of what the body should ideally look like – in terms of weight, shape, and so on – that is perpetrated and ensconced in the social order by real images of bodies (in magazines, movies, etc.). Presenting an appropriate body image to peers is now a widespread obsession of adolescents. That is why dress, hairstyle, and facial decoration are so critical during adolescence. Those who are unsuccessful in constructing an appropriate image to suit peer expectations can end up doing great harm to themselves. Most 'get through it,' as the expression goes, but a substantial number of others do not, as the increase in eating disorders among adolescents over the past few decades clearly indicates.

The notion of an ideal 'look' can be extended as well to facial appearance and, thus, to the widespread use of cosmetics to enhance facial features in specific ways. Cosmetics have a long and unbroken connection with coming-of-age and fertility customs that go back considerably in time. As anthropologist Helen Fisher has documented, even in the prehistoric Cro-Magnon era, during the last glacial age, pubescent tribal members apparently spent hours decorating themselves, plaiting their hair, donning garlands of flowers, wearing bracelets and pendants, and decorating their tunics and leggings with multi-coloured fur, feathers, and beads.[1] They did this to celebrate the advent of physical maturity, with the endorsement and approbation of the elders. The hair dyes, tattoos, and rings people put on their ears, noses, lips, eyebrows, and tongues are modern-day derivatives of these tribal courtship props – they are props used to stage a sexually appropriate character for peer audiences.

The use of cosmetics outside coming-of-age rituals also has precedents. But the history books reveal that it was largely the privilege of aristocrats. As such, it was viewed sceptically and critically by the masses, who saw it as an extravagance of the pampered and the spoiled. Among the earliest records of cosmetic use in ancient civilizations are artifacts from the First Dynasty of Egypt (c. 3100–2907 B.C.) in the form of unguent jars, some of them scented, found in the tombs of that era. They were probably used by both wealthy men and women to keep their skin supple and unwrinkled in the dry heat of Egypt. The well-off women of Egypt also developed the art of eye beautification by applying dark-green colour to the under-lid and by blackening the eyelashes and eyelids with kohl, a preparation made from antimony or soot. Similar kinds of cosmetics were in wide use among patrician women in the Roman Empire. In their beauty-enhancing arsenal they had rouge, depilatories, kohl, chalk for whitening the complexion, and pumice for cleaning the teeth. Members of the nobility in ancient Mesopotamia and Persia also indulged in cosmetics and fashion. The males curled, dyed, and plaited their long hair and beards, sometimes adding gold dust or gold and silver ornaments to it for embellishment.[2]

As an aside, I mention that the body has always been viewed as a moral, social, and aesthetic symbol in cultures throughout the world. In ancient Greece it was glorified as a source of pleasure, in ancient Rome as the root of moral corruption, and in the Christian church as both a temple and an enemy of the soul. Since ancient times, Western philosophy has constantly debated the nature of the relation of the body to the soul and the mind. The French philosopher and mathematician René Descartes (1596–1650) even went so far as to suggest that God had created two classes of substance that make up the whole of reality – one was thinking substances, or *minds*, and the other was extended substances, or *bodies*.

The use of cosmetics and clothing styles by the masses for image-enhancing purposes surfaced in northern Italy in the late Middle Ages, when a system of social classes based on wealth, ancestry, and occupation emerged. People wore certain styles of clothing to identify themselves as members of a particular class. Before the late Middle Ages, only wealthy and powerful individuals concerned themselves with such class-conscious matters. But when the class system developed, the general population began to compete for positions within society. New styles were still set by monarchs and prominent personages, but were spread by travellers, by descriptions in letters, and by the exchange of fashion dolls. The first fashion magazine is thought to have originated around 1586 in Frankfurt, Germany. It became so popular that it gradually replaced fashion dolls.

One of the first true 'fashion crazes' surfaced among young Italian men during the Renaissance. While the elders of the era dressed in traditional long robes, the new generation of young males began wearing tights and shorts, as well as close-fitting jackets called doublets. The spread of that fashion craze, however, was short-lived and highly limited in its territorial scope. In actual fact, before the nineteenth century, fashion for the masses was looked upon with a cynical eye as being silly and socially useless. For this reason, regulations called sumptuary laws were passed in many parts of Europe. They were designed to control the amount of money people could spend on private luxuries, thus preserving divisions among the classes and regulating fashion according to a person's rank in society. In some countries, only the ruling classes could legally wear silk, fur, and other expensive fabrics and materials. But the lure of fashion caused many people to break such laws.

The spread of commercially manufactured cosmetics to all classes gained momentum in the nineteenth century after the French made more and better cosmetics available at low cost. At the same time, industrialization had put more money into the pockets of common folk. At the start of the twentieth century, dressing and looking fashionable was becoming more and more a requirement of middle-class bourgeois life – a trend already satirized by Molière (1622–73) two centuries earlier in his masterpiece *Le bourgeois gentilhomme* (1670). The play mocks a successful but naïve cloth merchant who dons aristocratic clothing and simulates aristocratic manners and discourse in the hope of being received at court. Molière would, no doubt, have a field day satirizing current fashion trends in society! In his darkest ironic imagination, he could never have seen that society would have become a 'communal *bourgeois gentilhomme*.'

The extent to which people will go nowadays to 'look the look' is mind-boggling. Take tattooing as an example. Tattooing was practised by the Egyptians as early as 2000 B.C. to indicate social rank, affiliation, or allegiance – some historians date it even farther back in time by several millennia. Sailors introduced the practice into Europe during the Age of Exploration (in the sixteenth and seventeenth centuries). Throughout the twentieth century in North America, Australia, New Zealand, and Europe, tattooing remained popular among sailors. But near the end of the century, the practice gained popularity with people from all walks of life, including fashion models, youth gangs, and prison inmates. It was propelled into mainstream American culture in 1981 by the Rolling Stones album *Tattoo You* – an album that sold millions and became one of the most popular rock albums of all time. Today, tattooing has become body fashion for one and all. A fifteen-year-old can show his tattoos alongside an eighty-year-old and cause little or no comment.

Sensitivity to body image starts generally at puberty; but in our image-conscious world, it may crystallize long before that. It is not unusual, in fact, to find tweenies as young as seven or eight who are as conscious about how they look as are fourteen- and fifteen-year-olds. The difference, of course, is that tweenies are essentially still children engaging in make-believe; teenagers, on the other hand, are the real thing. Wanting to deflect attention away from themselves, adolescents resort typically to various cosmetic and clothing strategies that are designed to hide or masquerade obesity, facial blemishes, and various other perceived flaws in body image. On the other hand, they may opt for cosmetic alterations and clothing styles that convey a counter-culture persona. Interestingly, in the late 1990s more and more females adopted a 'tough look,' similar to the one expected of their male counterparts in previous eras. But, in my view, that trend was hardly an act of defiance against traditional gender roles. Rather, it was, and continues to be as I write, a general symptomatic response to media images. The new 'girl power' look was promulgated by media personages such as the Spice Girls and Britney Spears and by TV and movie characters such as Xena (the Warrior Princess), la Femme Nikita, Lara Croft, and Charlie's Angels (to mention but a few).[3] Women warriors and fearless individuals are also spotlighted on TV programs such as *The Fear Factor* – where women are as reckless as their male counterparts in putting themselves through inane physical trials to test their 'fear factor.' At the same time, the media have also perpetrated a more 'foppish' male body image through TV and movie characters. Vanity is gender neutral. The success of unisex fragrances such as Calvin Klein's CK, and of unisex stores such as the Gap, Banana Republic, and Abercrombie and Fitch, has made that transparently obvious.

The blurring of differences in body image can be called *de-gendering*. The roots of this phenomenon can be traced to the first decades of the twentieth century, becoming a major impetus for social change in the hippie 1960s. In the 1930s, females started wearing pants as part of an emerging de-gendering trend. But it was a short-lived one. With the counter-culture movement, however, women wore pants regularly, not as a fashion statement, but as a political one, with the underlying subtext of gender equality. Today, the wearing of pants is no longer perceived in de-gendering terms. The symbolism of de-gendering is to be found instead in other unisex trends, such as tattooing and body piercing. It is particularly noticeable in the girl-power images that the media promote – images exploited by psychologists, as well, to promote and define a new femininity based on 'solid psychological principles.'[4] Movies and television programs now show more female actors in the roles of warriors, heroes, and martial-arts experts than ever before. Girl power has become the norm, ironically modelled after male aggressive behaviour. From TV wrestling matches to workout programs, females are portrayed as being as powerful as males, if not more so. This new pattern of groupthink spawned a new literary genre at the end of the millennium known as 'Chick Lit,' which deals with the consequences of de-gendering from the female point of view. The genre revolves around twenty- to thirty-year-old urban females who have high-paying careers in big cities, and who are perpetually in search of the 'perfect guy,' who, of course, does not exist. The subtext of the narrative is fairly obvious – females can survive without marriage.

De-gendering has also led many females to adopt behaviours that were once expected to be primarily characteristic of males. For example, the smoking of cigarettes and the social use of drugs became genderless in the hippie 1960s. And aspects of sexuality that were considered to be part of male behaviour also became genderless in that era. Today, the sex seekers and the initiators of courtship can be male or female, with no one taking any notice of the gender of the seeker or the initiator.

But gendered coolness still exists – whether or not we are conscious of it – and is spread primarily through the media. In the 1950s, 'cool' male teens modelled themselves after Elvis Presley, a look recycled by the television character known as 'The Fonz' on the 1970s sitcom *Happy Days*. In the 1960s, the cool look was revamped to reflect the clothing and hairstyles worn by the Beatles; in the 1970s and 1980s, it ranged from a Madonna-type look for females and a John-Travolta-disco-type look for males to a punk look for both males and females. Alongside such trends, a 'surfer' look associated with certain movie and television teen stars of that era also became popular. In the 1990s, a hip-hop form of coolness emerged alongside a Latino form, with the rise of popularity of both hip-hop and Hispanic pop music – a form that was highly sensitive to gender. In both cases, the powerful sexuality of the female body was emphasized through clothing and cosmetics.

As can be inferred from the above sketch, the only constant in coolness is inconstancy. But certain things seem to remain basic. One of these is 'toughness.' When cool teens walk together on a city street in view of others, they tend to stroll along slowly and menacingly, crossing an intersection sluggishly and defiantly ignoring traffic signals. They walk and look as if they had a proverbial 'chip on their shoulders.' They are sending out the message 'Don't mess with us, unless you want to rumble!' That kind of behaviour encapsulates what it means to be 'street cool.' Unnoticed coolness has no value whatsoever. Coolness is meant to be observed and to cause a reaction.

Coolness varies, assuming different labels. *Ravers*, for instance, engage in raves (concerts-cum-dances at which recreational drugs are consumed). *Hip-hoppers* and *gangstas* assume the dress styles and brash attitudes of rap and hip-hop artists. Sometimes, the need to assume a 'tough cool' look leads an adolescent to seek membership in a gang. Social scientific theories on the causes of gang membership focus on background influences. Some suggest that teens engage in criminal behaviour because they were not sufficiently penalized for previous delinquent acts or because they have learned criminal behaviour through interactions with others. Others posit that teens commit crimes out of frustration with their low socio-economic status, or as a repudiation of middle-class values. There is an element of truth in all such theories, of course. In my view, however, the most powerful factor in the teen's decision to join a gang is, simply, that it is cool. Glorified by movies and music videos, gang membership affords many teens the opportunity to look and act tough *just for the sake of it* or, more accurately, *for the look of it*. One thinks, for instance, of the media mythologization of ghetto teen gangs in the 1950s – a phenomenon captured brilliantly by American composer Leonard Bernstein (1918–90), lyricist Stephen Sondheim (1930–), and librettist Arthur Laurents (1918–) in their 1957 musical *West Side Story*. Today, joining gangs is no longer characteristic only of teens who live in ghettolike districts of urban centres. It cuts across all sociocultural, socio-economic, and regional lines. The reason for this, in my view, is the psychological impact that the 'tough cool look' has on the adolescent's world-view. Psychologists who explore family background or socio-economic variables to find the causes underlying the increase in violence among teens are, more often than not, barking up the wrong tree. The power of gang symbolism, with its tribal connotations, has probably much more to do with teen violence today than any of the traditionally accepted social causes.[5] In this area of teen behaviour, too, de-gendering has taken full effect. Girls today are as prone to join gangs as are boys. And their behaviour may be just as violent.

Fashion Rules

A sure sign that the FYS has become widespread is the fact that the names of fashion designers are as well known as those of artists and intellectuals (if not better known). Fashion models are contemporary icons of beauty. Hordes of people aspire to look and dress exactly like them. Fashion shows are part of the everyday scene. Fashion magazines fill the shelves of stores. And, like everything else in our neomaniacal society, the turnover in fashion trends is rapid and constant. It is no exaggeration to say that today *fashion rules*! As discussed above, in the past fashion was the concern primarily of the aristocracy; the clothing of ordinary people changed far less radically. But even among the upper classes, clothing was costly enough to be cared for, altered, turned inside out and reused, and passed from one generation to the next. Neomania in fashion surfaced for the first time after the Industrial Revolution, which made the production of both cloth and clothing far easier and less expensive. Today, the close alliance of the garment and advertising industries has, in effect, killed fashion in its traditional sense and replaced it with what can only be called faddism. Many cultural historians believe that the last real attempt at true fashion was the 'New Look' of the late 1940s and early 1950s, which was, in retrospect, really no more than an attempt to retreat from the horrors of the Second World War.

There is little doubt that the media–entertainment industry has been the primary means of spreading faddism among teenagers. Take, for example, blue jeans. People began wearing blue jeans in the 1850s when Levi Strauss and Company sold tough cotton work pants to gold miners in California. At that time, jeans were perceived to be work clothing. They became fashionable among young men on college campuses in the 1940s and 1950s, and even more so when actors Marlon Brando (in *The Wild One*, 1954) and James Dean (in *Rebel without a Cause*, 1955) wore them on screen. In the counter-culture 1960s, young people wore blue jeans to symbolize rebellious political and social beliefs. Televisions across the world showed them in jeans taking part in civil rights marches and antiwar protests. Sales boomed as a consequence. By the mid-1970s, jeans had evolved into a fashion statement, becoming expensive, exclusive, often personalized, and available mainly at chic boutiques. Today, blue jeans are no big deal. They are items in a culture-wide wardrobe that is ageless and genderless. Everyone wears them, from two-year-olds to ninety-year-olds. Unlike in previous eras, when someone past the age of sixteen who wore jeans would have been perceived as confused or eccentric, today they are worn by anyone of any age without attracting the slightest critical comment.

As mentioned above, the de-gendering process has, paradoxically, not done away with gender distinctions. For example, blouses that allow females to put their cleavage on display made a 'comeback' in the late 1990s – I characterize it as a 'comeback' because that fashion trend was not unlike the one of wearing sexy corsets in the eighteenth century. And, needless to say, female sexuality is being constantly spotlighted by the media. It is everywhere, from movies such as *Lara Croft: Tomb Raider* (2000) and *Charlie's Angels* (2000) to World Wrestling Federation (WWF) television spectacles where busty females parade their mammary assets in front of drooling male audiences. Even the titles of some current women's magazines highlight sexual prowess – *Bust*, *Moxie*, *Bitch*, *Bamboo Girl*, *Hip Mama*, and *Rockrgrl*, to name a few. In such magazines, lipstick and liberation are discussed in the same paragraph. But some levelling of the sexual playing field has been taking place. Male sexuality, too, is being spotlighted as never before by the media, ranging from the Latino look *à la* Ricky Martin to the hip-hop look of Eminem and company. Significantly, in our forever young culture, such fashion trends pass quickly into the mainstream. The manufacturer Tommy Hilfiger, for example, actively embraced hip-hop fashion in the late 1990s, spreading it to other age groups.

Sexual images are everywhere. It is, by the way, of little use to censor such images, as some right-wing U.S. politicians are attempting to do. Censorship has never worked. It is based on the assumption that children and adolescents must be protected from 'indecent' information – whether in art, literature, or on a Web site – that might harm their development. Where does this assumption come from? Children experiment sexually with each other all the time. It comes from our romantic view of childhood as 'innocent' and 'pure' – no more, no less.[6] When I was a child of barely five, I remember being extremely interested in female anatomy and found a willing partner to show it to me. Of course, she asked me to show her my own anatomy. Where did we get this 'obscene' need from? The media? Hardly.

Clothing constitutes a symbolic force field. Most young people can explain how their clothing reflects their beliefs, their values, and those of their peer group. But they are rarely aware of the hidden symbolism of the clothing items they put on. Few modern-day punks, for instance, know the story behind the wearing of leather collars with sharp spikes protruding from them. Such spikes were once used for dog training. They protruded inwards, so that if a command was disobeyed, the dog's leash, attached to its collar, would be pulled. This was designed to punish the dog by driving the spikes into its neck. Through such negative conditioning, the dog gradually learned to obey commands. Being against all forms of authority and social conditioning, the early punks reversed the dog collar in parody of such obedience training. The protruding spikes, therefore, symbolized a reversal of power alignments. They signalled that the wearer would never be controlled by society. The type of clothing that early punks donned was *confrontation dressing*. Its main characteristic inhered in transforming everyday objects, such as collars, into fashion items so as to subvert their original social meanings. Razor blades, tampons, and clothes-pegs used as 'jewellery' were other examples of the confrontational use of fashion items. Significantly, none of those interviewed by my research team who defined themselves as punks showed any awareness of this symbolism.

Given its symbolic power, juvenile fashion has become very big business. According to a 2001 survey by the Chicago-based marketing company Teen Research Unlimited, in the year 2000 American teens spent an astronomical $155 billion on clothes, cosmetics, and personal maintenance. At the same time, they persuaded their parents to spend another $100 billion. Many of today's parents behave more like friends than custodians, eager to share fashion experiences with their teen sons and daughters. Not only do they act like pals to their teens, they also look more and more like them. The generation gap seems to have been bridged by a common pursuit of the same fashion ideal. Leather hip huggers and midriff-baring tops were designed in the late 1990s for tweenies and their mothers alike. Everyone, it seems, has embraced faddism and its forever young subtext.

The history of youth dress styles since the mid-1950s is the history of our culture. In the 1950s, tight slacks, push-up bras, bobby socks, and bikinis characterized the female dress code, while motorcycle jackets, blousey shirts, and pencil-thin slacks typified the corresponding male code. The hippie 1960s were characterized by unisex clothing. Males and females alike wore ripped, tattered, and colourful jeans, along with long hair and sandals, to emphasize rebellion against the establishment, free love, sexual equality, and ecological harmony. In the 1970s, two main fashion codes emerged. One was the disco code; the other was the punk code. Disco fashion celebrated sexuality and fun; the punk code emphasized degradation and depravity. Disco males wore bell-bottoms, open shirts, and slick hair; disco females wore slinky dresses, long hair, and high heels. The punk costume was genderless. Punk hairstyles ranged from shaved heads to wild-looking hairdos of every colour imaginable; the punk code included army boots and leather jackets. But before long, disco and punk fashions faded. They gave way to the refined, clean-cut look of *preppie* teens on the one hand, and the menacing motorcycle-gang appearance of *hard rockers* (with their ripped jeans, leather boots, jackets, and T-shirts) on the other. By the mid-1990s the 'gangsta look' of *rappers* (with their hooded jackets, multiple earrings, oversized baggy jeans, and unlaced sneakers) came to the forefront.

It is safe to say that appearance has become an obsession. The number of teenage girls who are having breast implants to increase the size of their breasts is alarming, to say the least. And it seems to come, more often than not, with parental approval. Have we as a society created notions of beauty that leave teens with no other choice than to alter their bodies drastically? A recent Pennsylvania State University study (2001) found that boys and girls as young as five were suffering from problems with body image. Clearly, something is amiss. Some adolescents become so concerned about weight control that they end up victims of anorexia nervosa, in a drastic attempt to keep their weight down. Others overeat and then force themselves to vomit to avoid gaining weight. They are known as bulimics. Adolescents with such eating disorders have an extremely disturbed sense of body image. They see themselves as overweight when they are actually underweight. Significantly, anorexia and bulimia were virtually non-existent in children under ten a few years ago. Today, cases are cropping up in children as young as five or six![7] This is compelling evidence of how emotionally powerful the slim and lean look perpetrated by media images has become. The concern over virtually every facet of body image, from hairstyle to body shape, is a clear signal that we may have invested much too much meaning in looks.

It was once believed that such disorders were more common in North America and Western Europe than in other parts of the world, and that they were more prevalent among the prosperous and well educated. However, research in the late 1990s found them to be spread among all social and economic levels, and to crop up in many countries throughout the world. The juvenilization of the globe has brought about a concomitant spread of culture-based diseases as well. The myth of Narcissus now echoes ominously in all four corners of the global village.

Sex Sells

The images of sexiness are everywhere. On television and in magazines, sex sells clothes, cosmetics, hair cream, or whatever else is necessary to appear young and attractive.

Our current fixation with sex is, in part, a reaction against its prohibition by the Puritan founders of our society. The first sign of this reaction can be traced to the fascination with jazz culture that young people developed in the 1930s. In that era, the expression *cool cat* was coined to convey the sexual appeal that a jazz musician exuded. The increase in smoking among young people was a second sign of the growing desire to express sexuality openly. The two were intertwined. Smoking was an intrinsic part of the jazz night-club scene – a sexually symbolic act captured memorably on film by Gjon Mili in his 1945 movie, *Jammin' the Blues*. In the opening scene, there is a close-up of the great saxophonist Lester Young inserting a cigarette gingerly into his mouth, then dangling it between his index and middle fingers as he plays a slow, soft, hazy kind of jazz for the late-night audience. That scene oozed 'sexual cool.'

The sexual subtleties of the club scene were also captured magnificently by Michael Curtiz in his 1942 movie, *Casablanca*. Cigarettes and high fashion are the dominant visual features of Humphrey Bogart's (Rick's) café, suggesting the presence of a 'sexual charge' in the people hanging around in the café, quietly involved in late-night foreplay. There is a particularly memorable incident at the start of the movie. Swaggering imperiously in his realm, cigarette in hand, Bogart goes up to the character named Yvonne, expressing concern over the fact that she has had too much to drink. Dressed in a white tuxedo jacket, like a knight in shining armour, Bogart approaches his paramour, sending her home to sober up. As he talks to her, he takes out another cigarette from a package, inserting it deftly between his lips. He lights it, letting it dangle from the side of his mouth. So captivating was this image to young cinema-goers, that it became an instant standard of male cool imitated by hordes of aspiring male courtiers throughout society. In a scene in Jean Luc Godard's *Breathless* (1959), Jean-Paul Belmondo stares at a poster of Bogart in a movie theatre window display. He takes out a cigarette and starts smoking it, imitating Bogart's mannerisms in *Casablanca*. With the cigarette dangling from the side of his mouth, the tough-looking Belmondo approaches his female partner with a blunt 'Sleep with me tonight?' The parody is unmistakable.

The makers of Camel cigarettes strategically revived the 'Casablanca scene' in their advertising campaigns of the early 1990s, through the images of a camel dressed in an elegant evening jacket, smoking, and playing the piano in a club setting, a cigarette dangling suggestively from the side of his mouth.

Smoking retains its sexual connotations to this day. And indeed, most of the teens interviewed by the research team (nearly 78 per cent) perceived cigarettes as sexual accessories. No wonder, then, that campaigns by concerned groups to dissuade teens from smoking have had little success. Smoking has become, since the 1930s, what anthropologists call a memorate – an unconscious communal thought pattern that impels people to interpret smoking in sexual terms. Cigarettes are popular among teens because they are *sexy*.

The history of smoking shows that tobacco has been perceived at times as a desirable thing and at others as a forbidden fruit.[8] But in almost every era, as Richard Klein[9] has eloquently argued, cigarettes have had some connection to sex, or to something that is erotically, socially, or intellectually appealing. Musicians smoke; intellectuals smoke; artists smoke. Smoking is a symbol of both sexuality and unabashed bravado. Movies tell us that smoking is a prelude to sex and a form of relaxation afterwards; smoking seems to be the entire point of being an adult; smoking is fun. As Michael Starr puts it, 'smoking is, in many situations, a species of rhetoric signifying certain qualities of the smoker.'[10]

Sexual images in the media are powerful because they are memorates. They impel people to perceive certain looks, clothes, and objects as sexy; others as not. Nature creates sex; culture creates sexiness. There are no universals in what constitutes sexual attractiveness; nor are there universals in the area of courtship. It is informative to note that the word *sex* comes from the Latin *secare* ('to section, divide'), suggesting that the Western memorate of sexuality was fashioned by the ancient myth of Hermaphrodite, the peculiar creature with two faces, two sets of limbs, and one large body. Hermaphrodite was resented by the gods, who ended up dividing her into two biologically separate sections – male and female. Western civilization has, ever since, focused on differences between the sexes rather than on similarities, even though there are probably more of the latter.

In our forever young world, sex-seeking has become ageless and genderless, as mentioned above. Media images impel all of us, no matter who we are, to seek sex. For our quest to be successful, the same images inform us how to dress and look. By rubbing Oil of Olay cream on her face, the mature woman of today can remain forever young and sexually appealing; by dabbing on Grecian Formula, and thus disguising his white hair, the mature man of today can likewise remain young looking and appealing. Maintaining a youthful, sexy appearance has itself become a memorate. It is what makes lifestyle advertising effective; and it is (on the brighter side) what can revive a marriage that has become stale. It is also the reason why even people in their sixties, seventies, and eighties continue to 'date.' The number of senior singles age fifty-five and up rose by 27 per cent from 1996 to 2000.[11] For the fifty-plus crowd, there are now a host of dating services with truly revealing names such as Cupid's Couch (Los Angeles), Great Expectations (Dallas), 92nd Street Y 60+ Program (New York), Match.com (Dallas), Warner Historic Hotels (Hertfordshire, England). Clearly, dating and sex are not for the pubescent only. These have become patterns throughout the modern life cycle.

The fixation on sex and dating would also explain the astonishing popularity of TV dating programs, with names such as *Blind Date, Change of Heart, Date Plate, A Dating Story, Dismissed, Elimidate, Ex-Treme Dating, The 5th Wheel, Love by Design,* and *Shipmates.* These programs emphasize instant fame, near-instant sex, and a little money on the side – all characteristic features of the FYS. In a society that has devalued the family as a locus for courtship, it should come as no surprise that the appurtenant rituals are showcased on programs such as *Meet My Folks*, in which suitors are grilled by Mom and Dad using a lie detector.

A Two-Edged Sword

In our forever young world, maintaining a sexy appearance is as much cultural pattern as it is biological drive. But this pattern is a two-edged sword. It is clearly a good thing to be in a position finally to unshackle all the ridiculous restrictions and taboos with regard to sex that the Puritan founders of our society held to be so sacrosanct. That view was not only silly, it was downright dangerous, as the great American novelist Nathaniel Hawthorne (1804–64) showed in his penetrating novel *The Scarlet Letter* (1859). The novel is about an adulterous Puritan, Hester Prynne, who is 'branded' a sinner. Through her story, Hawthorne laid bare the sheer folly of the Puritan view of sex. However, the current fixation with sexual appeal impels many people, young and old, to go to the other extreme – that of striving to look sexy and fashionable no matter what the cost.

In all fairness, the Puritans were not the only ones who had a restrictive view of sex. Such a view is actually quite widespread even today, in both our own and other cultures. As the late French philosopher Michel Foucault (1926–84) argued, the sexual body has always been a point of contention in human history.[12] What a specific age or society defines as 'sins of the flesh' is hardly universal. The Puritans saw any form of sex outside marriage as sinful. They also prohibited any expression or representation (verbal or non-verbal) that alluded to sex, because they feared that it would encourage sinful sex. Many current-day conservative politicians are just as fearful, as they patronizingly condemn 'obscene materials' and Hollywood's 'lack of morals.' On the other hand, there are many hedonistic traditions in our own and other cultures that exalt and glorify the eroticism of the human body. The art of strip-tease is a case in point. Obviously, what is 'obscene' behaviour to some is 'natural' behaviour to others. While sexual urges are based in biology, perceptions of what is or is not sinful are ensconced in cultural traditions and habits.

The history of the modern cosmetics industry is a perfect example of the two-edged nature of the FYS. Many condemn the rampant use of cosmetics as a narcissistic disease spread by the beauty industry and the media working in concert. While this may be true to a large extent, it is also true that cosmetics have been useful socially, as Kathy Peiss has recently argued in her interesting book on the cosmetics industry.[13] Simply put, cosmetics have liberated women to express their sexuality – something that tends to be strictly forbidden by religious people. The founders and early leaders of the 'cosmetics movement' were simple women: Elizabeth Arden (1884–1966), a Canadian, was the daughter of poor tenant farmers; Helena Rubinstein (1870–1965) was born of poor Jewish parents in Poland; and Madam C.J. Walker (1867–1919) was born to former slaves in Louisiana. While it is true that our media culture preys on social fears associated with 'bad complexions,' 'aging,' and so on, it has at the same time allowed women to assert their right to emphasize their sexuality, not conceal it.

As I mentioned earlier, in my view there is little point in proposing drastic measures to censor or repress media images of any kind. For one thing, such measures are effective only if individuals are already predisposed towards their content; for another, media moguls will always find ways around such measures. In early 1998, the U.S. Congress banned the Joe Camel and Marlboro Man figures from cigarette advertising. In response, ad creators came up with ingenious alternatives. In a later 1998 ad campaign, Salem cigarettes used a pair of peppers curled together to look like a pair of lips, with a cigarette dangling from them. Benson and Hedges ads in the same year portrayed cigarettes as people – floating in swimming pools, lounging in armchairs, and so on. As it turned out, this new 'government-permissible' form of advertising was even more effective in suggesting the glamour and pleasure of smoking than the figure of Joe Camel had been, as witnessed by a significant rise in smoking among teenagers from 1999 to 2000 (according to national surveys published in newspapers and magazines at the time).

The advertisers' images are persuasive because they are based on communal memorates. They have become so familiar that we no longer question them. That was the worrisome theme of *The Hidden Persuaders*, Vance Packard's 1957 book on the subliminal effects of advertising.[14] The debate on advertising that his argument generated is beyond the scope of my book; suffice it to say that the images and rhetoric of advertising have become part of modern groupthink – even if we are critical of them. As J.B. Twitchell aptly puts it, 'language about products and services has pretty much replaced language about all other subjects.'[15] We assimilate and react to advertising images unwittingly and in ways that parallel how individuals and groups have responded in the past to religious images and icons. Advertising has become one of the most ubiquitous, all-encompassing modes of expression ever devised by humans. As McLuhan quipped, the medium in this case has indeed become the message.[16] There are now even Web sites, such as AdCritic.com, and TV programs that feature ads for their own sake, so that audiences can view them for their aesthetic qualities alone.

Subliminal messages about the quest for beauty and the conquest of death are constantly being built into the specific images that advertisers create for certain products.[17] Advertisers now offer the same kinds of promise and hope to which religions and social philosophies once held exclusive rights – security against the hazards of old age, better positions in life, popularity and personal prestige, social advancement, better health, happiness, and so on. In a phrase, the modern advertiser stresses not the product but the social and personal benefits that are supposed to ensue from its purchase. As Naomi Klein has emphasized, our 'logo' culture creates images of lifestyle that now shape the fabric of our groupthink.[18] One pattern in this fabric is a blurring of the categories of young and old. The fashion trends of the young are recycled and marketed as the fashion styles of all; and the fluctuating aesthetics of the youth culture are quickly absorbed by society at large.

Perhaps, like Faust (1480?–1540?), the legendary German fortune-teller and magician, we want to cheat death through the illusion of remaining young. Faust – the story goes – made an agreement with the Devil to trade his soul for occult knowledge of magic and for twenty-four years of pleasure and power. At the end of the twenty-four years the Devil carried Faust off to hell. Faust then repented the bargain, but it was too late. Is faddishness the work of the Devil, as some now think (literally)? I do not think so. Remaining in the realm of mythology, it is more accurate to call it the work of Nemesis, who has made narcissism a way of life, thus surreptitiously transforming us into little more than the clothes we wear. As the great novelist Virginia Woolf (1882–1941) remarked in her 1928 novel, *Orlando*: 'There is much to support the view that it is clothes that wear us, and not we, them; we may make them take the mould of arm or breast, but they mould our hearts, our brains, our tongues to their liking.'[19]

What our culture desperately needs, in my view, is to recover the 'naked' beauty that the human face and the human body have *on their own*. That is something that the great visual artists have attempted to do throughout history and across cultures. The face is a metonym of our humanity. The portraits of artists are symbolic probes of the face. They are powerful interpretations of the many meanings that life etches into the 'human mask.' In our narcissistic culture we seem to have forgotten the lessons that Sandro Botticelli, Leonardo da Vinci, Raphael, Titian, Vincent Van Gogh, and many others taught us a long time ago. They explored the 'poetry' of the face, seeking to extract from its expressions of sadness, humour, joy, and tragedy the meaning of life itself. A cosmetically altered appearance modelled after the images found in fashion magazines is hardly an attempt to capture what is meaningful or beautiful about the face. The faces of fashion models in magazines are devoid of all emotion.

In no way do I wish to imply that photography is incapable of capturing the naked beauty and emotional nuances of the face. On the contrary, I mention the photographic art of Dorothea Lange (1895–1965). Lange was among the first to exploit the photograph's power to portray the poignancy of the faces of real people in unadorned settings in the 1930s. Diane Arbus (1923–71), too, used photography to capture the ebb and flow of impressions, feelings, and thoughts registered by the human face, transforming the inner lives of human beings, and their otherwise average circumstances, into extraordinary events. The paradox of our contemporary culture lies in the fact that the photographs of Lange and Arbus are sold in bookstores alongside those of fashion photographers whose photographs are intended merely to convey cool.

CHAPTER THREE

Talking like Teenagers

Language most shews a man: Speak, that I may see thee.

Ben Jonson (1573–1637)

As trivial as it may sometimes seem, human talk provides a critical window into the nature of the conceptual system of the talkers and the culture in which they were reared. As the American anthropologist Edward Sapir (1884–1939) emphasized throughout his career, we are, essentially, what we speak.[1] Sapir's pupil, Benjamin Lee Whorf (1897–1941), went so far as to claim that thought systems themselves are built into the very structure of languages. In effect, if such scholars are right, language constitutes a mental template through which people come to perceive and understand the world.[2]

The Sapir–Whorf perspective raises some fundamental questions about the connection between culture and language. Do terms such as *chairman* or *spokesman* predispose speakers of English to view social roles as gender-specific? Feminist social critics think so. They maintain that English grammar is organized from the perspective of those at the centre of the society – the men. That is why, not long ago, we would tend to say commonly that a woman 'married into' a man's family; and why, at traditional wedding ceremonies, expressions such as 'I pronounce you man and wife' were (and continue to be) common. Such linguistic habits define women in relation to men. Others, such as 'lady atheist' or 'lesbian doctor,' are exclusionary of women, since they insinuate that atheists and doctors are not typically female or lesbian. In the Iroquois language, the reverse is true – the grammar of Iroquois is organized from the perspective of the women. That is because in Iroquois society the women are in charge – they hold the land, pass it on to their heirs in the female line, are responsible for agricultural production, control the wealth, arrange marriages, and so on.

The foregoing discussion is meant to suggest that language puts on display trends in a culture that tend to go unnoticed because they are implicit in the categories of the language itself. Today, many of those categories are derived from youth slang. Although slang is very old, it is unprecedented, to the best of my knowledge, that an entire culture takes many of its discourse cues from youth-generated slang. Words such as *loony, nuts, psycho, babe, chick, squeeze, dude, sloshed, plastered, make out, scram, split, chill,* and many more, have become so much a part of our everyday vocabulary that we hardly ever realize that we have taken them from teen slang. Adolescent slang is everywhere, alongside adolescent fashions and lifestyles. As the American poet Kenneth Rexroth (1905–82) has aptly put it, 'When the newspapers have got nothing else to talk about, they cut loose on the young. The young are always news. If they are up to something, that's news. If they aren't, that's news too.'[3]

In all previous eras, the mannerisms of speech manifested by young people were hardly considered to be worthy of emulation. Indeed, the contrary was true. Young people were expected to adopt adult forms of grammar and vocabulary. But today, the reverse seems to be the case. Proper usage has gone out the window with the fashions of the old, and canons of verbal style are now shaped by the ever-changing categories of youth slang. My objective in this chapter is to discuss this very intriguing (albeit somewhat worrisome) symptom of the FYS.

Slang Rules

Slang rules common discourse today, not because it is any better or worse than the standard language, but because it is everywhere. In order to understand why, it is necessary to take a close look, first, at the nature of adolescent slang itself,[4] given especially that talk during adolescence seems to be of paramount importance. As Neil Howe and William Strauss report in their book *Millennials Rising: The Next Great Generation,*[5] talking occupies most of the teen's time (on the phone, in electronic chat rooms, etc.). The following figures taken from a late 1990s survey by Reed Larson of the University of Illinois at Urbana-Champaign make this saliently obvious:

*How does the average teen spend time when not at school or doing home-
work (per day)?*

Talking	120–180 minutes
TV viewing	90–180 minutes
Paid labour	40–60 minutes
Sports	30–60 minutes
Household chores	20–40 minutes
Clubs, the arts	10–20 minutes

The language spoken in a society is rarely homogeneous, especially
in large societies like our own. Certain people or groups within the society may use, on a regular basis, a version of the language called slang,
which implies the use of non-standard words and phrases, generally
shorter lived than the expressions of ordinary colloquial speech. I
should emphasize from the outset, however, that slang is hardly 'vulgar' speech (note that originally *vulgar* meant 'of the common people');
rather, it constitutes a powerful form of discourse because it bestows a
recognizable identity on its users, since certain attitudes and values of
the group are built directly into the structure, meanings, and modes of
delivery of slang words and phrases. Moreover, slang is not a corruption of the standard language. It is, simply, a version that can be put to
any use its speakers desire. Should the need arise to create a new word
category, all a slang speaker has to do is be consistent with the structural
requirements of the language's sound and grammar systems. The word
itself will do the rest, calling into existence its referent. In conducting
research in the early 1990s, I recall asking a teenager what the word *dork*
meant. At the time, *dork* had not gained the currency that it enjoys
today. She defined a dork as 'a greasy male teen, who studies chemistry
all night.' I had certainly seen such boys, but I had not thought of them
as belonging to a category. I simply viewed them as studious, but
unpopular, teens. I knew of no word in the English language, previous
to hearing *dork*, that called attention to them as such. But after learning
what *dork* meant, I suddenly started seeing dorks everywhere, eventually believing that the dork category did indeed have a *raison d'être*.

We often do not realize that many terms we use commonly started
out as slang – the word *jazz*, for example, was originally slang for
'sexual intercourse.' Slang finds its way into the cultural mainstream

in many ways. In the past, its primary conduits were great writers. Shakespeare, for instance, brought into acceptable usage such slang terms as *hubbub, to bump,* and *to dwindle.* But not before the second half of the twentieth century did it become routine for the conduit to be teenagers. For instance, the words *pot* and *marijuana,* which were part of a secret criminal jargon in the 1940s, became common words in the 1960s after they were adopted by the counter-culture youth of the era. The number of such words that have entered the communal lexicon since the 1960s is immeasurable.

The slang of adolescents is, in a way, quite different from other kinds of slang. It constitutes a kind of social dialect with specific traits that set it apart from adult forms of slang. For this reason, I suggested the term *pubilect* ('the dialect of puberty') in 1994 to designate it.[6] Whatever one calls it, teen slang provides an outlet for adolescents to express in their own terms the whole gamut of emotions they feel.[7] It is a high-energy and emotive code. This can be seen, for instance, in the tendency of adolescents to stress their words with exaggerated carica-ture – 'He's sooooo cute!' 'She's faaaaar out!' 'That's amaaaazing!' Its emotivity also surfaces in the kinds of intonation patterns that teens typically utilize, such as the following one built into various kinds of utterances – 'We called her up (?) (intonation like a question) ... but, like, she wasn't there (?) (same pattern) ... so we, like, hung up (?) (same pattern).' Colloquially named 'uptalk' by the media, this pat-tern is actually an implicit *tag questioning* strategy. A *tag* is a word, phrase, or clause added to a sentence to seek approval or to ascertain some reaction – 'She's coming tomorrow, *isn't she?*' 'That was a good meal, *right?*' Uptalk is, in effect, a tag question without the tag, indi-cating an unconscious need to ensure the full participation of in-terlocutors, to seek their approval, and to enact emotions verbally. Inci-dentally, as I write I notice that this feature is on its way out, as new generations of teens adopt different modes of delivery.

Perhaps the most outstanding feature of teen slang is the presence of so many descriptive words in it, most of which have been coined to mock, shock, or satirize. In the mid-1980s, words such as *loser, gross out, airhead,* and *slime-bucket,* for instance, were in widespread use in North American pubilect. In the 1990s, *vomatose, thicko, burger-brain,* and *knob* gained currency. Regardless of the generation, however, the motivation behind the coinage of such words is the same. They are products of an unconscious need to describe others and meaningful social situations in ironic ways, so as to deflect attention away from oneself. Irony is absent from child language. Before puberty, the child uses language to understand the world and the people in it, not to critique it. In child-hood, language is a 'tool of knowledge.' At puberty, however, the ado-lescent comes to realize that language can be used as another kind of tool – namely, a 'weapon' that can be employed to defend oneself or to attack someone else. The ironic weaponry of adolescent slang can be clearly seen in words such as *megabitch, geek, party animal, dog* ('unat-tractive person'), and *wimp dog* ('male with little personality'). Even the humour that such words generate is rooted in irony. Expressions such as *MLA = massive lip action* ('passionate kissing'), *barf* ('vomit'), and *blimp boat* ('obese person'), which were in vogue in the early 1990s, never fail to evoke a kind of sardonic chortle or snicker that only irony can elicit. Many jokes, cracks, witticisms, and quips produce a similar effect. Together, they constitute an arsenal of highly effective and ver-satile verbal weaponry.

But there is not one single arsenal; there are many. Each one is spe-cific to a particular lifestyle. In the 1980s, members of hard-rocker cliques, for instance, used obscenities and vulgarisms regularly to con-vey toughness; in the 1990s, many teens adopted hip-hop idioms to convey the same kind of street toughness and savvy (real or implied). As the American author and critic Elizabeth Hardwick has put it, 'The language of the younger generation has the brutality of the city and an assertion of threatening power at hand. It is military, theatrical, and at its most coherent probably a lasting repudiation of empty courtesy and bureaucratic euphemism.'[8]

Slang rules the domain of teen discourse because it provides the means to assert oneself in social settings in a way that is often brutal but always creative and witty. As the American poet Carl Sandburg (1878–1967) put it, 'Slang is a language that rolls up its sleeves, spits on its hands and goes to work.'[9] Interestingly, as many teen words pass on to the adult domain of discourse – I mention *dork* and *geek* as cases in point – they lose their original ironic content, or at least impact. Like some of the clothing items of the punks, which lost their original sub-versive connotations when they were adopted by the adult world, so too most slang words lose much of their 'military, theatrical' force, as Hardwick describes it, when they are uttered by adults.

Cool Talk

Slang, like teen music and fashion trends, is highly unstable, continu-ally changing from one teen generation to the next. But certain tend-encies and patterns remain constant across generations. First and foremost, the ways in which teenagers deliver their messages orally is, as mentioned above, guided constantly by emotivity. When teenagers utter expressions such as 'Awesome!,' 'Neat-oh!,' or 'Ohmygod!' with prolonged stress, accompanying gesticulations, facial contortions, and so on, they are drawing attention to their feelings and moods through the semantic and intonational qualities of the words and phrases. Such expressions and modes of delivery are, however, hardly limited to the adolescent domain. Through constant exposure in movies and on television, and through their utilization by celebrities, they have crept into common discourse. An expression such as 'Ohmygod!' has become so commonplace that we hardly realize that it comes from the teen domain of discourse. The same applies to the misuses of *like*, which now reverberate throughout adult conversations. In teen discourse, this simple word first emerged as a strategy for showing hesitation and uncertainty, giving teen speakers time to put words to ideas without losing input in a communicative situation: 'I, like, wanna come, but, like, I'm a little busy now.'[10] It is very difficult to interrupt the flow of speech when *like* is being used in this way. *Like* is also used to carry the implicit meaning *Are you listening to me? Don't you agree?* 'Like, you know what I mean? It's, like, you said, and, like, I said too.' It also provides speakers with a simple means to soften the negative impact of an opinion: 'I think the song is, like, bad.' This is less harsh and confrontational than saying flatly, 'The song stinks.' *Like* also affords interlocutors an indirect means to satirize or critique someone or something: 'He was, like, a real loser, like a freak, man!' Finally, *like* is commonly used as a quotative. A *quotative* is an expression, such as 'she said' or 'he repeated,' followed by a quotation. In teen discourse, *like* has replaced most quotatives: 'Sherry was, like, What are you doing?' in place of 'Sherry said, What are you doing?' The use of *like* as a quotative is traceable to the so-called Valley Girl talk of the early 1980s. The inaneness of such talk was captured masterfully by the late Frank Zappa in his 1982 song 'Valley Girl,' in which he parodies the use of *like* and other mannerisms of the era. By the way, I discovered recently in the discourse of the *Scooby Doo* cartoon characters a use of *like* as a quotative and hesitation mannerism that goes back to the late 1960s. This suggests that these functions were already present in the pubilect of the hippie era.

The use of *like* as a quotative now permeates oral adult discourse. Everywhere one turns, one hears expressions such as 'She's, like, I don't care,' rather than 'She said, I don't care.' And, given its ubiquity, it comes as little surprise to find that it is also taking on various other grammatical functions in adult grammar. For example, it is replacing *that* in utterances such as 'I feel like he wants it, rather than 'I feel that he wants it.' Interestingly, some of the slang uses of *like* have precedents. A check of the *Oxford English Dictionary* will reveal, in fact, that the use of *like* meaning 'in a way, so to speak' (as in, 'I'm, like, so in the mood') goes back to 1778. However, most of its current functions are the products of teen pubilect.

During the mid-1990s, the word *duh* gained circulation among teens as a counterpart to *like* – a word likely modelled on Homer Simpson's *D'oh!* expression. With its perfectly paired linguistic partner, *Yeah-right*, it crystallized to provide the means for both understatement and overstatement at once. *Duh* is a tool of wry savvy and sarcasm. In 1999, I asked a fifteen-year-old boy 'Don't you think it's a great day today?' His answer was a blunt 'Duh,' indicating ironically to me the futility of my comment. It was equivalent to saying, 'Tell me something I don't know.' *Duh* is assertive, a perfect tool for undercutting mindless chatter or insulting repetition.

Today, *duh* and *like* can be detected everywhere in the media and in conversations between people of all ages, at the same time that the new teen generation seeks replacements for them. The use of *man* tells a similar semantic story. Expressions such as 'That guy's a loser, man,' 'I'm so hammered, man, I think I'm going to heave,' 'He's seriously wasted, man,' became common in male teen slang in the early 1980s. In that era, *man* clearly functioned as a gendered code word for male teens. It spoke of male bonding, fellowship, and 'buddyism.' Today it has gained currency with both genders and, significantly, with speakers of all ages. It has become a general strategy for expressing buddyism in all kinds of situations. It is now ageless and genderless.

When considered as a whole, the words, strategies, and tactics of teen slang constitute a grammar of cool. Cool talk, like cool fashion, is 'in' (pardon my slang). It can be heard on television, in movies, and in street talk. But among teens, cool talk, like cool clothes, varies constantly. The following excerpt, taken from a 1999 recording session made at a Toronto high school, will give the reader a flavour of cool talk in one of its many versions:

Male adolescent A:	Yo, whassup?
Male adolescent B:	Not much, man, like, whassup with you?
Male adolescent A:	Ya still makin' out with that hottie ('good-looking girl')?
Male adolescent B:	Na,' she's no mint chick ('good person'); she gives

	ya headbubbles ('a headache'). But I'm still dealing with her ('going out with her').
Male adolescent A:	Straight up ('really')?
Male adolescent B:	What about you, dude?
Male adolescent A:	I'm, like, cool. I'm still chillin' out over my last hot-tie. She was nasty. But nobody plays with me ('fools around with me').

The above dialogue reveals how cool talk constitutes a means for building ironic content into the structure of interactions. Many of the forms and expressions used are self-explanatory. Others require a glossary, even if they are grafted from the existing resources of the standard language.

Slang forms are derived in various ways. Here are some of them:

- Recycling words through abbreviation
  bod ('body')
  bro ('brother, friend')
  delish ('delicious')
  hyper ('hyperactive')
  non preesh ('I do not appreciate')
  rad ('radical')

- Combining words
  check out ('look at, examine')
  chill out ('relax, do nothing')
  diss on ('criticize, belittle')
  geekdom ('world of geeks')
  hold out ('wait')

- Assembling existing words or parts of words to create new ones
  megabitch ('very troublesome female')
  shitface ('shit' + 'face')
  vomatose ('vomit' + 'comatose')

- Creating acronyms or abbreviations
  24/7 ('all the time,' acronym for twenty-four hours a day, seven days a week)
  5–0 ('police,' derived from the television series *Hawaii Five-0*)
  BTW ('by the way')
  DL ('down low' = 'secret')
  GMO ('get me out')

L ('liquor store')
MLA ('massive lip action' = 'passionate kissing')
TSH ('that shit happens')
Y & R ('young and restless')

- Forming words onomatopoeically
  barf ('vomit')
  josing ('craving')
  ralph ('vomit')
  skank ('promiscuous female')

- Rhyming
  bad rad ('good party person')
  sight delight ('good-looking male')

- Altering the meaning of existing words
  awesome ('great')
  bad ('good')
  bomb ('great')
  bones ('money')
  boss ('excellent')
  cool ('nice, great, good, attractive')
  diva ('with style')
  easy ('flexible, not difficult to please')
  excellent ('fine, OK')
  hottie ('good-looking girl')
  hurting ('acting silly')
  millers ('earrings')
  mint ('cool, good-looking')
  player ('promiscuous male')
  radical ('wild at a party')
  rap ('talk seriously')
  shooter ('liar')
  sweet ('good-looking')
  tight ('difficult person')
  wicked ('excellent')

- Adopting forms from pop music
  bummer ('bad experience')
  Whassup? (from hip-hop)
  Yo (greeting expression from hip-hop)

As these examples make clear, cool talk allows teens to draw verbal pictures of others, make condensed commentaries on significant events in their social lives, and satirize situations that are meaningful to them, *and to them alone*. Each coinage is, arguably, comparable to a small poem, since it is designed to convey an experience, an idea, or an emotion in a way that is more concentrated, imaginative, and powerful than ordinary speech. Each construction brings one literally 'into the social heart' of teen life, providing a poetic insight into how the average teen experiences that life.[11]

As already intimated, it is the 'ironic intellect' that reigns supreme in slang coinages. The following words and expressions, which were recorded by the research team in 2000 and 2001, will give the reader some idea of how this form of intellect manifests itself through slang, producing expressions that are humorous, critical, friendly, and descriptive all wrapped into one:

- *all about that* ('favour')
- *anyway* ('goodbye')
- *babe* ('good-looking guy')
- *bag it* ('forget about it')
- *ballin'* ('flaunting money')
- *beats* ('music')
- *bitch out* ('yell at')
- *bud, chronic, herbals, ish, nuggets, smoke, trees issues* ('marijuana')
- *chick flick* ('sentimental movie,' indicating that it is a genre watched by female teens)
- *chill* ('relax')
- *crib* ('home,' implying the childish treatment teens receive at home)
- *ditz* ('good-looking but clumsy girl')
- *dope* ('excellent')
- *flintstones* ('older people, especially parents')
- *fly, killer, lethal, gone, hammered, wasted* ('drunk')
- *fresh* ('cool')
- *gank* ('break up')
- *gnarly* ('gross/cool')
- *grub* ('food')
- *hardcore* ('extreme')
- *heated* ('angry')
- *hittin' it, rukin,' slammin,' blessin' it, stylin' it, taggin' it* ('having sex')

- *hot box* ('stolen car')
- *I'm ghost, jet, bounce, flex, outee* ('I'm leaving')
- *issues* ('personal problems')
- *it's all good* ('it's cool')
- *jacked, buff, cut, diesel, deeze, ripped* ('muscular')
- *jawsin'* ('talking')
- *kiss-up* ('opportunist')
- *later, peace out* ('goodbye')
- *lit, baked, blazed, blitted, blunted, fried, lifted* ('inebriated, drugged out')
- *lynched* ('falsely blamed')
- *mad* ('very much,' as in 'He's making mad loot at that job.')
- *minute* ('a long while,' as in 'Where you been? I haven't seen you in a minute.')
- *peep this* ('listen to this')
- *popo* ('police')
- *props* ('respect,' as in 'You get mad props for that.')
- *rad* ('cool')
- *rag on* ('make fun of')
- *random* ('odd,' as in 'There were some random guys at that party.')
- *run* (suggesting that drinking liquor is illegal and thus must be obtained illegally, as if on the run)
- *scrub* ('ill-mannered')
- *shotgun* ('front passenger seat')
- *skater* ('rock aficionado')
- *sketch out* ('act strangely')
- *sketchy* ('weird, shady')
- *step to* ('challenge')
- *stoner* ('druggie')
- *sucks* ('unpleasant, awful')
- *sweat* ('desire,' as in 'She sweats me.')
- *tooled on* ('roughed up')
- *whack* ('screwed up')
- *whip, ride* ('car')

Such coinages constitute verbal tools that allow the speaker to make an indirect commentary on a situation, without elaboration or justification. This is especially noticeable in terms coined to refer to body image, appearance, peer personality types, and recreational social activities. The following examples are comparable, in effect, to one- or two-word jokes about people or specific aspects of everyday life, since they refer to them in much the same ways as a satirist would.

- *biffed* ('crashed')
- *burbulating* ('relaxing')
- *busted* ('ugly female')
- *butt* ('ugly')
- *chunk* ('obese')
- *dick* ('unfair')
- *epic* ('a long ride')
- *fly girl* ('party girl')
- *grille* ('face')
- *nasty* ('unattractive,' or its opposite, 'attractive')
- *sperm donor* ('a father who's never around')
- *stain* ('useless person')

The use of ironic metaphor is another strategy of teens for communicating their own perspective. Some metaphors are harsh, providing strength and intensity; others are smooth, providing finesse to the commentary. This double texture of slang is especially noticeable in the domain of sex:

- *bombs* ('female breasts')
- *booty* ('rugged female')
- *cannons* ('female breasts')
- *dip* ('girlfriend')
- *gettin' nice* ('going steady')
- *hittin' it* ('having sex')
- *player* ('promiscuous male')
- *skank* ('promiscuous female')

Ironic metaphor also underlies the coinage of words referring to personality types. The following are cases in point; their meanings are self-evident.

- *acid head*
- *airhead*
- *bougie*
- *burger brain*

- *dexter*
- *dickhead*
- *dildo*
- *dingo*
- *dirt ball*
- *dodo*
- *douche bag*
- *dozy*
- *drip*
- *dude*
- *dweeb*
- *flea bag*
- *freak, goof*
- *greaser*
- *Guido*
- *motor head*
- *peabrain*
- *rah-rah*
- *redneck*
- *squid*
- *thicko*
- *wimp*

A few years ago, I collected some truly interesting data that showed how highly versatile such a strategy is in adolescent slang. I simply asked several teenage females in a Toronto high school how they would describe males in their school whom they found to be cool or attractive, by completing the sentence 'He's ...' Here's a sampling of the responses I got:[12]

- 'He's nasty,' 'He's bad' = ironic depiction of the negative effect the male teen is perceived to make on females
- 'He's a stag,' 'He's a catch' = perception of the male teen as a desirable sexual animal
- 'He's a Ferrari,' 'He's Park Avenue' = perception of the male teen as a rare or admirable object, entity, or place
- 'He's hot,' 'He sizzles' = perception of the male teen in terms of sexually stimulating bodily states
- 'He's full of beef,' 'He's a stud muffin' = perception of the male teen as a food item, implying a desire to eat him sexually

- 'He's chiselled,' 'He's a fine piece' = perception of the male teen as a work of art

Actually, as Alice Deignan (among many others) has recently argued, such metaphorical strategies are hardly restricted to adolescent slang; they are general verbal strategies that allow people to encode subjective judgments in a way that is meant to conceal their very subjectivity: 'Speakers use a metaphorical expression to encode their approval, or – far more frequently – their disapproval, of a manifestation of desire. The evaluation, thereby, takes on the appearance of objectivity.'[13] Nor are such strategies peculiar to speakers of English. There are, in fact, many cross-cultural similarities in the ways in which sexual attractiveness and desire are modelled metaphorically. In the Chagga tribe of Tanzania, for example, the perception of sex and love as things that can be tasted manifests itself constantly in discourse about romance. In that society, a young man is perceived to be the 'eater' and the young woman his 'sweet food,' as can be inferred from everyday expressions that mean, in translated form, 'Does she taste sweet?' 'She tastes sweet as sugar honey.' Such a remarkable correspondence suggests that this particular perception of sexuality and attractiveness probably cuts across cultures and age. But what is perhaps unique about the metaphorical coinages of contemporary adolescents is their all-pervasiveness and their utilization to depict a particular world of its own.[14]

This world is captured rather cleverly in the language used by the characters on the hit teen TV series *Buffy the Vampire Slayer*. On that program, new terms and phrases have been coined on nearly every episode, many of them formed in the usual ways, some of them at the crest of new formative tendencies. Known as 'slayer slang,' it constitutes a particularly vivid snapshot of contemporary American teen slang. And, far from being ephemeral vocabulary, slayer slang is steadily intruding on everyday speech and may be here to stay. Expressions such as 'My egg went postal on me,' 'What's up with that?,' 'Wow, you're a dish,' 'Doesn't Owen realize he's hitting a major backspace by hanging out with that loser?,' and so on, have come from slayer slang. For the teens on that program, as for teens worldwide, it serves as a transgressive code. Meaning, then, is sometimes difficult to isolate, but not the sociolinguistic importance of the slang words.

Particularly cool in the late 1990s were expressions from hip-hop culture. Their omnipresence in teen discourse revealed how dominant the adolescent segment of pop culture has become in shaping all kinds of trends. With the images of street toughness and blatant sexuality that hip-hop and rap videos put on daily display, it is little wonder that many teens became swayed by the 'talk' of the characters on those videos. The following examples give some idea of the kinds of words and expressions that became widespread as a result of the influence of the hip-hop scene on late 1990s teens:

- *411* ('information,' as in: 'What's the 411 on him?')
- *all that* ('in possession of all good qualities')
- *baller* ('basketball player,' 'successful person')
- *battle* ('to compete')
- *B-boy* (from 'break boy,' meaning 'one who breakdances')
- *beats* ('music')
- *benjamins* ('dollars,' after the picture of Benjamin Franklin on paper currency)
- *blower* ('the telephone')
- *boo* ('term of endearment,' as in 'She leaves school early to see her boo.')
- *butter* ('smooth, nice,' as in 'That's a butter jacket.')
- *cheddar* ('money')
- *come correct* ('to be genuine')
- *digits* ('phone number')
- *dis* (short for 'disrespect')
- *dog* ('buddy,' 'friend,' indicating the perception of dogs as loyal)
- *down low* ('quiet, secret,' as in 'They kept their marriage plans on the down low for months.')
- *down with* ('to be sympathetic towards someone')
- *flavour* ('style,' as in 'He has mad flavour.')
- *fly* ('attractive')
- *front* ('pretending,' as in 'He's unpopular 'cause he's always frontin.')
- *gangsta* ('gang member')
- *get on* ('to do something well')
- *homeboy/homegirl* ('close friend')
- *hyped* ('cute')
- *ill* ('to be obnoxious')
- *jiggy* ('to be rich')

- *keepin' it real* ('staying cool')
- *mack* ('pimp')
- *mad* ('beautiful')
- *peep* ('look at,' as in 'Did you peep the Knicks game last night?')
- *peep, crew, posse* ('friends, people')
- *phat, sweet, nice, ill* ('superb')
- *played* ('used, dumped,' as in 'You really got played by your man.')
- *player* ('promiscuous male')
- *recognize* ('take notice of,' as in 'You'd better recognize, or you're history.')
- *represent* ('do something well,' as in 'Michael Jordan represents on the basketball court.')
- *run* ('buy liquor')
- *shorty* ('girlfriend')
- *slamming* ('attractive')
- *tag* ('a person's graffiti nickname')
- *tenda* ('girlfriend')
- *tool* ('someone trying hard to belong')
- *whassup?* ('hello')
- *word* ('truth')
- *yo* ('hello')

Above all else, these words reveal the conceptual system that teens utilize to interact with each other. In data collected in 2002, expressions such as the following show very clearly how teens think about things and, more importantly, each other. They provide descriptive detail of the mental images that go through the adolescent's mind on a day-to-day basis.

- *bender* ('someone who is sad')
- *bent* ('upset')
- *blaze* ('smoke up')
- *bo* ('girlfriend')
- *book it* ('let's go')
- *bottled* ('drunk')
- *bredgrin* ('a friend')
- *bucket-o-solid* ('you are ugly')
- *chillax* ('chill out' + 'relax')
- *chopping* ('flirting')
- *dime* ('a joint')

- *facing* ('kissing')
- *floater* ('someone who listens to all types of music')
- *fronting* ('flirting')
- *fun bags* ('breasts')
- *geevin'* ('don't care')
- *ghetto clothes* ('stylish clothes')
- *gnarly* ('cool')
- *hoes* ('loose girls')
- *hottie* ('cute guy / cute girl')
- *ill* ('cool / good')
- *ill* ('that's stupid')
- *josing* ('craving')
- *peaked* ('ugly')
- *purple monkey* ('sex')
- *ralph* ('vomit' and 'idiot')
- *raver* ('someone who wears baggy clothes and large necklaces, does drugs, goes to overnight parties, and listens to techno music')
- *rockers* ('those who like rock music and wear dark clothes')
- *shooter* ('show off')
- *sick* ('cool / good')
- *skaters* ('those who wear baggy clothes and have many piercings')
- *solid* ('amazing, cool, great')
- *spun* ('crazy, lost')
- *tank* ('someone who is strong')
- *wigger* ('wannabe thug')

Many of these have gone out of style as I write, or are about to do so. Ephemerality is, in fact, the defining feature of teen slang. Ironically, the coinages that do survive are those that are adopted by the adult world: for example, *24/7* and *Ohmygod* are now commonly used by people of all ages, being piped into society on a daily basis through movies, TV programs, advertisements and commercials, and other channels of pop culture. As a result, adult language is becoming increasingly more juvenilized, changing and adapting in response to adolescent categories and styles of talk. Teen words of a few years ago, such as *cool, nerd, dork,* and *geek,* have even been listed in standard dictionaries of the English language, such as the *Oxford Dictionary* and *Webster's,* as have more recent words such as *gangsta, phat, D'oh!* (Homer Simpson's expression, which is a variant of Duh!), *24/7* ('all the time'), *easy* ('see you later'), *floss* ('to show off, brag'), *ice* ('diamonds set in platinum'), *mad* ('anything to its extreme'), and *tight* ('to be broke'). The juvenilization of language, like that of fashion, has become a wide-spread phenomenon indeed.

Spreading the Word

Before his death, Marshall McLuhan claimed that electronic media would have a substantial impact in shaping the course of civilization in the twenty-first century. He argued this on the basis of the human historical record. He noted that major shifts in cultures were marked not by political or military events but by the medium in which information was recorded and transmitted.[15] His main argument was a simple but insightful one. He remarked, for example, that the shift from a tribal to an urban form of life came about because of the spread of alphabets. These made print the basis on which people conducted their affairs, replacing the 'word-of-mouth' mode of tribal cultures. It was the ancient Phoenicians who first compiled an abstract system of alphabet characters for recording the consonant sounds that made up words. The Greeks adopted the Phoenician alphabet and introduced characters for vowel sounds, thus producing the first true alphabet, in the modern sense of the word.

McLuhan also believed that electronic literacy would eventually take over from print literacy in creating a true global village. In this village, the world's languages would merge in various ways, especially in how they encoded thoughts and ideas. McLuhan's prophetic view rings especially true in the domain of teen slang. In this village, the concepts expressed by one teen slang coincide with those encoded by another. Pubilect has become the Esperanto of the modern world, uniting people across the globe in a bizarre adolescent way. In research I conducted in Italy on teen slang in the 1990s, I found, in fact, a remarkable pattern of similarity between Italian and North American slang.[16] For instance, I noticed the exact same tendency to convey emotivity through intensified language markers. The specific manifestation of this pattern inheres in the tendency of Italian youth to overly prolong tonic vowels:

- *Che beeeello!* ('How nice!')
- *Stupeeeendoooo!* ('Great!')
- *Ma coooome?* ('What do you mean?')
- *Hei, ma sei un macaaaacco, eh?* ('You're a jerk, ya' know?')

Emotivity and irony are also conveyed by the use of

- interjections and exclamations
  Hei, cosa succede? ('Hey, what's happening?')
  Boh, e chi ci capisce niente? ('Duh, who can figure it out?')
  Ah-oh, ma che cacchio fai? ('Duh, what the heck are you doing?')

- swear words
  Hei, cazzone, che fai? ('Hey, big prick, what are you doing?')
  Sei proprio un leccamerda. ('You're a real ass-licker.')

- *cioè*, which is the Italian equivalent of *like*
  L'ho chiamato, cioè, a casa, cioè, quando non c'era lei, cioè, ... ('Like, I called him up, like, at home, like, when she wasn't in, like ...')

Italian pubilect also reveals the presence of uptalk. This surfaces in two main ways:

- as an *eh* tag
  Allora ti piace, eh? ('So, you like it, huh?')
  No, no, eh, non è mica vero, eh? ('No way, huh, it's not true, huh?')
- as a hesitation groan, *mmmmm*, that is interjected throughout the sentence
  Devo, mmmmm, dire che, mmmmm, non capisco, mmmmm. ('I have to, uhm, say, that I don't understand, uhm.')
  Io, mmmmm, penso, che quello là, mmmmm, è un cretino. ('I, uhm, think that that guy there is, uhm, an idiot.')

As in North American teen slang, irony guides the coinage of most of the new words and expressions:

- A *togo* is someone who was defined to me as *bello, stupendo, divertente* ('nice, stupendous, fun'); it is equivalent to English *cool*.
- A *grasta* is a female teen who is *cretina, stupida, scema* ('idiotic, stupid, loony'); it is equivalent to English *loser*.
- A *secchione* is someone who is *troppo studioso* ('too studious'); it is equivalent to English *dork* or *nerd*.

Other ironic coinages I recorded are self-explanatory. They reflect a creative use of the resources of the Italian language to portray people and events in ways that are practically identical to those used by North American teens:

- *Andiamo col tuo ferro, eh?* ('Shall we go with your iron?' = 'Shall we go with your car?')
- *una cabina* ('a person who wears designer clothing')
- *Camomillati!* ('Take chamomile!' = 'Cool it!')
- *Ci vai mai a scimmiare?* ('Do you ever go monkeying?' = 'Do you ever go dancing?')
- *Dammi un po' di ossigeno.* ('Give me some oxygen.' = 'Give me a cigarette.')
- *Devo andare in catalessi presto.* ('I have to go into catalepsy soon.' = 'I have to get some sleep soon.')
- *Fantasmati!* ('Become a ghost!' = 'Get out of here!')
- *fior di fragola* ('strawberry flower' = 'beautiful female')
- *ghignare* ('sneer' = 'laugh')
- *gli spinelli* ('sticks' = 'cigarettes')
- *il chiodo* ('nail' = 'a stupid person')
- *il cocomero* ('watermelon' = 'stupid')
- *il museo* ('the museum' = 'school')
- *la bestia* ('beast' = 'tall and big girl')
- *la caverna* ('the cave' = 'the home')
- *la chica* ('a female who wears baggy clothing, a ragazza rapper')
- *la ciste* ('cyst' = 'an ugly girl')
- *la cozza* ('an unattractive female')
- *la lingua* ('tongue' = 'kiss')
- *la paglia* ('straw' = 'cigarette')
- *l'erba* ('grass' = 'marijuana')
- *l'iceberg* ('iceberg' = 'wimp')
- *lo scocciofono* ('the ball-break-o-phone' = 'the telephone')
- *lo stregone* ('the witch doctor' = 'the doctor')
- *Loro si francobollano spesso.* ('They postage stamp each other frequently.' = 'They kiss a lot.')
- *Perché ti buchi sempre?* ('Why do you always prick yourself?' = 'Why do you always shoot up?')
- *schiodare* ('pull out a nail' = 'to pay off')
- *slegare* ('untie' = to dance')
- *sniffare* ('to sniff' = 'an anglicism')
- *Sono asfaltato.* ('I'm on the asphalt.' = 'I'm broke.')
- *stonato, tossico* ('stoned, toxic' = 'drugged out')

As in North America, Italian slang items have a very short lifespan.[17] By comparison with vocabulary change in the language as a whole, which sometimes takes centuries, the rate of change in teen vocabularies is greatly accelerated. Remarkably, some slang terms are gaining general currency in Italy, cutting across age boundaries. I have personally seen words such as *spinelli* ('cigarettes') and *ferro* ('car') used on advertising posters in various parts of the country. And the expression *Camomillati!* ('Cool it!') is now commonplace. As Teresa Labov has shown with her intriguing research, coinages have staying power and spread if they have what can be called a high 'aesthetic index,' appealing to our ironic and poetic instincts at once.[18] Needless to say, terms referring to sex seem to have a very high aesthetic index, in both English and Italian pubilect. The following metaphors for sexual parts and activities that I collected in Italy in the last few years are cases in point:

- *beccare* ('to peck' = 'to have sexual intercourse')
- *il bigolo* ('penis')
- *la canna* ('fishing rod' = 'penis')
- *il cavallo* ('horse' = 'penis')
- *dare dei colpi* ('to give bangs' = 'to have sexual intercourse')
- *farsi* ('to make oneself' = 'to masturbate')
- *il fiocco* ('knot' = 'kiss')
- *la lallera* ('vagina')
- *limonare* ('to kiss with the tongue')
- *menarsi* ('to lead oneself' = 'to masturbate')
- *il mostro* ('monster' = 'penis')
- *la pera* ('pear' = 'vagina')
- *la pippa* ('pipe' = 'penis')
- *la pista* ('landing strip' = 'vagina')
- *il provolone* ('a stud')
- *rompere* ('to break' = 'to have sexual intercourse')
- *l'uccello* ('bird' = 'penis')

In effect, wherever the global village exists – generally throughout Europe, Australia, New Zealand, Russia, and other industrialized countries – words coined by teens surface constantly in discourse; where it does not, there are no traces of them.

Screenspeak

Pop culture has always been a source for innovative language. The jazz subculture, for instance, was responsible for introducing words such as *hip*, *stylin'*, *cool*, and *groovy* into the standard language. These have now become part and parcel of common everyday vocabulary. Some words have more staying power than others – for example *cool*, *jock* ('athletic type'), and *chick* ('female teen') go back to the 1950s; *stoned* ('inebriated, drugged out') and *hip* come out of the 1960s; *wheels* ('car') and *bummer* ('unpleasant experience') have been around since the 1970s. In the 1990s, hip-hop culture supplanted both jazz and rock and roll as a fertile source of new vocabulary. Expressions such as *bad*, *chill*, and *nasty* come from that culture. Many of the slang words that make it into the mainstream tend, *tout court*, to have a pop-culture history behind them. Take *bad* as an example. Michael Jackson released his album *Bad* in 1987, starting a trend of using *bad* in a non-literal way (meaning 'attractive'). In 1989, hip-hop artist L.L. Cool J introduced the phrase *not bad* 'meaning bad, but bad meaning good,' as he defined it in his song 'I'm Bad.' The word *bad* has thus been passed on from one teen generation to the next, gaining general currency through the conduit of pop culture.

Of all the 'pipelines' in this conduit, cinema is the one that has played the most crucial role in spreading teen slang throughout society and the world. In a postscript to the published version of his play *Amadeus* – which became an Oscar-winning 1984 movie – British playwright Peter Shaffer (1926–) comments insightfully as follows:[19]

> The cinema is a worrying medium for the stage playwright to work in. Its unverbal essence offers difficulties to anyone living largely by the spoken word. Increasingly, as American films grow ever more popular around the world, it is apparent that the most successful are being spoken in Screenspeak, a kind of cinematic esperanto equally comprehensible in Bogotá and Bulawayo. For example, dialogue in heavy-action pictures, horrific or intergalactic, now consists almost entirely of the alternation of two single words – a cry and a whisper – needing translation nowhere on the planet: *Lessgidowdaheer* and *Omygaad*.

'Screenspeak,' as Shaffer aptly designates it, has indeed become the koine of the global village. The way celebrities speak on the silver screen becomes, immediately thereafter, a model of how to speak on the streets. Screenspeak is like a computer virus; it has entered the global village's 'hard drive,' and is now extremely difficult to eradicate.

Screenspeak is genderless and ageless. However, in the teen world itself a hypocritical double standard still seems to persist. Girls who are aggressive in dating are called *sluts* (or other terms, as indicated above), with all the negative connotations that the word evokes, whereas boys are called *studs* or *players*, with all the positive connotations that such words encode. As one female teen said despondently to me during a recent interview, 'I change boyfriends a lot; everyone at school calls me a whore, a slut. But guys get away with it. They're called players or studs instead. You know what I mean?' For some reason, girls continue to be held more accountable than boys for their sexual activities, even though we live in an openly sexual culture. This attitude is changing rapidly, but there are still a few of the founding puritanical residues around.

Undoubtedly, holding on to the speech patterns of one's youth is something that is probably inevitable. As the American behavioural psychologist William James (1842–1910) so aptly put it, 'Hardly ever can a youth transferred to the society of his betters unlearn the nasality and other vices of speech bred in him by the associations of his growing years.'[20] In a phrase, adults tend to speak as they once did as adolescents. At no other time in history, however, have adults become so mesmerized by how young people speak. The always witty and acerbic Oscar Wilde (1854–1900) saw this as a basic flaw in the American character. He put it ironically as follows: 'In America the young are always ready to give to those who are older than themselves the full benefits of their inexperience.'[21] The implicit message in Wilde's perceptive remark is rather transparent. In other parts of the world, and even in many parts of America, past and present, the world-view that youth tends to express through its discourse is something that the 'wise elders' in societies across time have always looked upon with a grain of salt.

This in no way implies that the youth of today have nothing to say of lasting value. On the contrary, they have a lot to say. American authors Jack Kerouac (1922–69) and Allen Ginsberg (1926–97), for instance, produced their best writings as adolescents, becoming figureheads for a new generation of young writers in the 1950s known as the 'Beat Generation' – a movement that embodied the idealism of William Holden and the pop culture banalities of the era in a bizarre amalgamation. That was modern adolescence's first true narrative movement, reflecting its ambiguous nature, as William Burroughs (1914–) clearly implied in his reflections on Kerouac in 1985: 'Kerouac opened a million coffee bars and sold a million pairs of Levis to both sexes. Woodstock rises from his pages.'[22]

Throughout history, young people have been active shapers of literary traditions. In the Middle Ages, the great Italian poet Dante (1265–1321), influenced by the love pangs of youth (for his beloved Beatrice), created a poetic portrait of the human soul that speaks to us meaningfully to this day. Dante's *Divine Comedy* transcends time and space; it is literally *ageless*. The unconventional works of Beat writers, too, are ageless, reflecting a profound disaffection with contemporary society that everyone feels. Their writings are characterized by a raw, improvisational quality. In their verbal portraits, they drew on their personal adolescent experiences. The movement was centred in San Francisco and New York's Greenwich Village, and it revolved around poetry readings, jazz performances, coffee shops, and the City Lights bookstore in San Francisco, run by Lawrence Ferlinghetti (1919–), himself a leading poet of the movement. Incidentally, the term *Beat*, with its double connotation of downtrodden and beatific, was first used in this way by Kerouac about 1952.

Screenspeak is not the only form of discourse that dominates the intellectual airwaves. The language of the soul and the heart is still around, even if it is becoming increasingly difficult to locate. The British writer George Orwell (1903–50) was well aware of how the language a society uses reflects its ethos. In his great novel *Nineteen Eighty-four* (1949) he saw language as the primary key for unlocking how people and cultures think. The worst world in which one could possibly live, he emphasized, is one in which people turn instinctively to 'exhausted idioms' and trendy new words, yet end up saying virtually nothing of value. Only language that ennobles the human spirit will persist. Screenspeak will not.

CHAPTER FOUR

Grooving like Teenagers

The new sound-sphere is global. It ripples at great speed across languages, ideologies, frontiers and races. The economics of this musical esperanto is staggering. Rock and pop breed concentric worlds of fashion, setting and life-style. Popular music has brought with it sociologies of private and public manner, of group solidarity. The politics of Eden come loud.

George Steiner (1929–)

The word *grooving* came into wide circulation in the 1960s as a figure of speech describing perfectly the kind of slow, pulsating music that was played at counter-culture 'happenings' such as open-air rock concerts. It also described the kind of music that was played at 'flower-power' demonstrations, as the Beat poet Allen Ginsberg (1926–97) characterized the strategy of friendly cooperation that the early hippies showed at rallies. The 'flower children,' as they were called, advocated universal peace and love as antidotes to all the world's social and political ills. They carried or wore flowers to symbolize their viewpoint. They held hands and 'grooved' to the guitar music they played at their peaceful protests.

The 'grooving music' of the flower children was, in effect, music for the 'neck upwards,' in contrast to music 'for the neck downwards,' as the British rock guitarist Keith Richards (1943–) characterized 1950s rock and roll.[1] Today, the term *groovy music* is still used, but it has lost its flower-power connotations. It is used simply to describe any kind of music that is popular and cerebrally undemanding, even the music that Richards described as stimulating the anatomical regions below the neck. Like that seventy-year-old Deadhead I mentioned in the opening chapter, virtually everyone seems to be in a constant mood to groove, even if the music no longer has any flower-power symbolism built into it.

In a phrase, the music of youth has become the music of all. This is yet another symptom of the FYS (forever young syndrome). Music is the topic of this chapter. I dedicate it to that charming seventy-year-old Deadhead (wherever she may be).

Pop Music

The rise and spread of pop music started in the first decades of the twentieth century. By 'pop music' I am referring to the kind of music that is popular among all strata of society but which traces its origins to musical trends started by young people. *Ragtime, jazz,* and the *Charleston* were the first true pop-music crazes of the early decades of the twentieth century. By the 1930s, jazz gave way to *swing* music – a particular style of jazz that was made popular through radio and sound recordings. From 1935 to 1945, swing ushered in the 'big band era,' which ended shortly after the Second World War, although the influence of swing could still be heard in the so-called jump band rhythm-and-blues music of the 1940s; and its appeal continues uninterrupted in many 'neo-swing' styles to this day.

After the war, the hard-edged Chicago blues of Muddy Waters, along with the 'hard-country' style of Hank Williams, caught on with large radio audiences. In the mid-1950s, the most successful genre of pop music of the twentieth century came to centre stage. *Rock* grew out of the intermingling of several streams of postwar music styles – swing music, the blues, the gospel-based vocal-group style known as *doo wop*, the piano-based rhythmic style known as *boogie-woogie*, and the country-music style known as *honky-tonk*. Promoted by entrepreneurs such as Alan Freed – who coined the term *rock and roll* as a distinct commercial pop-music category – and recorded by small independent labels, rock was an unexpected success. The reason for this is now transparent – it appealed to a newly affluent adolescent audience in the mid-1950s.

The first true rock song is considered generally to be Elvis Presley's 'Good Rockin' Tonight,' which he recorded in 1954. In actual fact, it was a remake of Wynonie Harris's 1947 rendition of the song – an up-tempo blues number where the word *rock* is mentioned. Among the recordings that set the stage for rock and roll after Harris's pivotal recording are Rosetta Sharpe's 'Up above My Head' (1948), Pee Wee Cayton's 'Blues after Hours' (1948), James Moody's 'The Fuller Bop Man' (1949), the Delmore Brothers' 'Pan American Boogie' (1949), Hank Williams's 'Mind Your Own Business' (1949), Wild Bill Moore's 'Neck Bones and Collared Greens' (1951), Jackie Brenston's 'Rocket 88' (1951), and Lloyd Price's 'Lawdy Miss Clawdy' (1952). By the time Bill Haley and the Comets recorded 'Rock around the Clock' in 1955, rock music was acclaimed by young and old alike as the rhythmic soul of adolescence. Rock and roll was a style of music that 1950s teens could call theirs, *and theirs alone*. Haley's song was the theme song for *The Blackboard Jungle*, a 1955 motion picture about teenagers and the many problems associated with coming of age in that era. The song established rock and roll's reputation as the music of teen rebellion. Adults looked down upon it. Some even considered it to be the work of the Devil. Clearly, those adults were unaware that the roots of the 'Devil's music' were to be found in their own musical backyard. Unless their brand of music was classical, all adults of the era were aficionados of one or several of rock's creative sources – jazz, swing, country and western, gospel, honky-tonk, and so on. What obviously bothered the adults of the era was the blatant sexuality that rock conveyed – the unabashed sexuality of puberty.

The 'golden era' of rock and roll – defined by the 'sexually charged' recordings of Bill Haley, Chuck Berry, Fats Domino, Elvis Presley, Little Richard, Jerry Lee Lewis, and Buddy Holly – lasted from 1954 to 1959. Rock was about teenage sexuality, courtship, identity, personal freedom, and other issues that were (and continue to be) of central concern to adolescents. It was an 'up front' music, speaking directly to the sexual hormones. And it was great fun, documenting and guiding the ludicrous coming-of-age period of 1950s North America – an aspect of golden-age rock and roll captured nicely by the 1978 movie *Grease* (based on the 1972 musical of the same name).

Rock was promoted from the outset by all media, especially the cinema. The 1956 movie *Rock Rock Rock!* for instance, included acts by Chuck Berry and the Moonglows, and those of many other 1950s musical icons. It also featured an appearance by disc jockey Alan Freed. It was essentially a 'proto-rock video' of Bill Haley and the Comets singing their popular tunes. 'Rock, Bay, Rock It' (1957) and 'Go, Johnny, Go!' (1958), not to mention Elvis Presley's 'Jailhouse Rock' (1957), made it clear that rock and roll was a type of music that would not 'go away' quickly, as many adults anticipated. As Danny and the Juniors prophetically put it in their popular 1958 tune, 'Rock and roll is here to stay (it will never die)!'

By the 1960s, rock had spread to all corners of modern culture, developing new genres and styles of its own – Motown (the Supremes), surf (the Beach Boys), folk (Bob Dylan; the Kingston Trio; Peter, Paul, and Mary), and so on. The so-called British invasion of rock began in 1964 with the arrival of the Beatles in New York city. The British rock bands invigorated mainstream rock, largely by reinterpreting the early classics of American rock. However, each group developed a distinctive new style – the Beatles combined Chuck Berry's driving sound into a sophisticated new vigorous style (as can be heard in 'I Saw Her Standing There'); the Animals adopted a rhythm-and-blues style to produce a new, powerful, earthy sound (as in 'House of the Rising Sun'); and the Rolling Stones incorporated aspects of Chicago urban blues into their distinctive, thrusting sound (as in 'Satisfaction'). By mid-decade, rock had become the 'default' musical idiom of the global village; audiences for swing, jazz, and other pop-music genres declined considerably. In one short decade, rock – the 'Devil's music' – had made its way to centre stage. And it had become extraordinarily lucrative.

Attempts were even made to raise rock to the level of musical art. The Beatles, the Stones, Jimi Hendrix, Eric Clapton, Procol Harum, and many more American, Canadian, and British musicians wrote songs that captured the attention of musicologists and the conductors of symphony orchestras. At the same time, soul music, the successor to rhythm and blues, added a new kind of emotional force to pop music, growing out of the gospel-based performances of Aretha Franklin, the funk techniques of James Brown, and the soulful crooning of Marvin Gaye. Country-and-western music, too, combined elements of older forms of country and western with a new emphasis on youth issues. Johnny Cash and Waylon Jennings helped contribute to the rising popularity of such music. All the new music styles were cleverly managed by media moguls who understood the new juvenilized 'laws of the marketplace' perfectly.

This became especially evident in the 1970s, when glamorous superstars of rock played to massive crowds in sports arenas. A plethora of distinctive new styles – *disco, glam rock, punk rock, new wave, reggae, funk,* and so on – were pioneered by independent labels to capture a growing, but fragmented, market. However, by the end of the decade audiences for rock became extremely fragmented, making it much less profitable for record companies to sell rock to large audiences. The music industry became nervously cautious following a drop in sales of recorded music by almost $1 billion between 1978 and 1982 and a similarly precipitous decline in income from live concerts.

A number of factors contributed, however, to the economic revival of rock during the mid-1980s. The advent of the music video – marked by the debut in 1981 of Music Television (MTV), a twenty-four-hour music video channel – and the introduction of the digitally recorded compact disc in 1983 stimulated demand for popular music as never before. The video-album *Thriller* (1982) by Michael Jackson became the biggest-selling product in pop-music history up to that time, and it established the pattern by which record companies came to rely upon a few big hits to generate profits. Other successful musicians of the period included Bruce Springsteen, the working-class bar-band hero; the artist known as Prince, whose 1984 single 'When Doves Cry' was the first song in twenty years to have topped both the mainstream pop charts and the black music charts; and Madonna, the iconoclastic performer from a working-class background who transformed herself into a controversial 'sex-kitten' pop icon. Image-making had become the central strategy in the promotion of musical aesthetics.

Fragmentation continued to characterize the 1990s. Bands such as Blur, Oasis, Pearl Jam, R.E.M., and Radiohead carried on the counter-culture traditions of 1960s rock. But it was rap and hip-hop that came to the aesthetic and economic forefront. All other kinds of trends came and went literally overnight. A survey conducted by *USA Weekend* magazine in 2002 showed that hip-hop/rap was the most popular of all genres, followed by pop in that year. The breakdown of the survey is as follows:

If you had to choose just one type of music to listen to exclusively, which would it be?

Hip hop/Rap	27%
Pop	23%
Rock/Punk	17%
Alternative	7%
Christian/Gospel	6%
R & B	6%
Country	5%
Techno/House	4%
Jazz	1%
Other	4%

In the mix, jazz and even classical music made an unexpected come-back (albeit one of limited economic scope). The number of newly formed record labels devoted to reissuing the classical music repertoire on CD was unforeseeable. Their success was fuelled in large part by the repeated use of classical music by the movies. Labels such as Naxos and Chandos, for instance, became highly profitable. The renewed interest in jazz culminated in a brilliant ten-part documentary on American public television (PBS), by director Ken Burns, in early 2001. The main point made by the program was that the jazz phenomenon not only dictated all subsequent pop-music trends but was also a mirror of twentieth-century musical art. The TV program was followed by a coffee-table book, a DVD boxed set, a five-disc CD companion, and a special series of twenty-two essential jazz artist compilations.

Today, there are dozens of pop-music genres around, each with its own market segment and each one promoted by specific record labels and radio stations. At the same time, non-American pop-music styles have started finding their way to North American soil through satellite-TV exposure. The Argentine tango, for instance, which gained popularity in the 1910s, initiated crazes for Latin ballroom dancing in Paris, London, and New York city throughout the 1990s. The same success story applies to the revival of the Cuban rumba and mambo, both of which were popular in the 1930s. In the contemporary global village, recycling often outdoes invention. I should mention that, as I write, Indian film music, which is produced in studios in New Delhi and Mumbai, is being given more and more airtime in mainstream North American media. African music, too, is becoming somewhat popular with individual audiences. It includes a number of distinctive regional styles, such as the ju-ju music of Nigerian bandleader King Sunny Adé; central African *soukous*, a blend of indigenous songs and dance rhythms with Afro-Cuban music; and South African *Iscathamiya*, the Zulu choral singing style performed by Ladysmith Black Mambazo.

The list of new trends for specific audiences could go on and on. Never before has music of all types been so available to consumers of all tastes. From jazz to the latest teen music craze, the recording industry has literally brought music to the people. But in virtually all the music, the emphasis is on youth. The whole world seems to be in a forever young groove. That is why the expressions and themes that pop music expounds quickly pass into general discourse, and why the clothing fashions that pop musicians wear quickly become general fashion trends. Pop music has become an intrinsic part of modern-day aesthetics, thanks to the mass media. Even classical music has become a bizarre media-promoted genre of sorts. The *William Tell* overture gallop movement by the eighteenth-century opera composer Gioacchino Rossini (1792–1868), for instance, has become so closely linked with the *Lone Ranger* TV series of the 1950s that the two are hardly ever perceived as separate by those who grew up in that era; similarly, another Rossini overture, the one he composed for the opera *The Barber of Seville*, has become so closely associated with a famous *Bugs Bunny* cartoon that the two are now inseparable in many people's minds.

Rockin' and Rollin'

The swing music that became the rage between 1935 and 1945 appealed mainly to the young people of the era, who saw it as a way to survive the stark economic realities of the post-Depression world and the moral ravages of world war. The juvenilization of music became even more evident in the 1940s, when adolescent girls screamed at every performance of the 'crooner-swinger' Frank Sinatra. A little more than a decade later, the same type of screaming was evoked by the first rock stars.

As mentioned above, the birth of 'commercial rock' is usually traced to the 1955 hit song by Bill Haley and the Comets, 'Rock around the Clock'. The song made it obvious to all that adolescence had emerged as a social force to be reckoned with – it even provoked riots in south London on its original release. Rock musicians introduced clothing and hairstyle fashions, and started dance crazes. In 1956, Elvis Presley became the king of rock, after appearing on *The Ed Sullivan Show* before a national audience. Presley's 'Hound Dog' (1956) and 'All Shook Up' (1956), Little Richard's 'Tutti Frutti' (1955) and 'Lucille' (1957), and Chuck Berry's 'Maybellene' (1955) and 'Johnny B. Goode' (1958) established the main features of hard-rock style – loudness, hard-driving rhythms, and sexual lyrics. But all this did not last for very long. By the early 1960s, Elvis was dethroned. Rock and roll became a medium for expressing revolutionary social and political ideas. It was no longer just music 'to dance to' or 'to fall in love by.' The radical hippie movement of the mid-1960s was propelled by a new, more engaging type of rock and roll. Its artistic voices denounced apathy, warmongering, racism, stereotyping, and other social ills. By the end of the decade, it became obvious to society at large that the Devil's music had become

Plato's music – the type of subversive music that the Greek philosopher Plato feared would undermine social stability.

The Beatles' 1967 album, *Sgt. Pepper's Lonely Hearts Club Band*, established new standards for studio recording and helped perpetrate the image of the long-haired rock musician as a creative artist. Rock and roll was fast becoming a kind of Beat Generation code in the musical idiom, complete with hallucinogenic drugs, psychedelic art, light shows, and an emphasis on spontaneity and communitarian values. Musicians such as Jerry Garcia and the Grateful Dead, Jim Morrison and the Doors, and Frank Zappa developed a unique blend of complex harmonies, rhythms, and lyrics tying them to the new hippie lifestyle and its revolutionary ideology. Jimi Hendrix became an instant legend at the first large-scale rock festivals in the United States – Monterey Pop (1967) and Woodstock (1969) – with his agonized outcry against the 'establishment.' Soul music reinforced the hippie subtext that change was inevitable. Paradoxically, despite the 'anti-establishment' focus of all types of 1960s music, and the rejection of traditional bourgeois goals, musicians signed lucrative contracts with major recording companies!

The use of drugs and the smoking of cigarettes became *de rigueur* because of their association with the *verboten*. Drug taking and smoking cigarettes are what artists, criminals, and other asocial or eccentric people have always engaged in.[2] To this day, the young take drugs or smoke to show that they are 'chic,' not to seek a path to enlightenment. This is the legacy of the hippie generation. And any legislative attempt to eliminate smoking will be of no avail for this very reason. As Tara Parker-Pope aptly puts it, 'For 500 years, smokers and tobacco makers have risked torture and even death at the hands of tobacco's enemies, so it's unlikely that a bunch of lawyers and politicians and the looming threat of deadly disease will fell either the industry or the habit.'[3]

The movement to raise rock to a different level of artistry did not last long. It was characteristic primarily of the 1960s and early 1970s – a period that continues to this day to attract broad interest and appeal, as confirmed by a VH1 poll released in 2001. Of the 100 albums chosen by 500 journalists, music executives, and artists as the most influential and important of rock history, most were recorded in the 1960s and 1970s. The top one chosen was the 1966 *Revolver* album with which the Beatles initiated their experiment to transform the simple, hard-driving form of early rock into a serious genre. With a few exceptions – such as Nirvana's *Nevermind* album (1991), which came in second, Lauryn Hill's *The Miseducation of Lauryn Hill* album (1998), which came in thirty-seventh, and U2's *Achtung Baby* album (1991), which came in sixty-fifth – the majority of the albums selected were recorded during the counter-culture era. No albums from the golden era made it to the list, except for Elvis Presley's *Sun Sessions*, recorded in 1954–5, although the album was not released until 1976. It was rated twenty-first. Dominating the list are the Beatles, the Rolling Stones, Bob Dylan, Led Zeppelin, the Who, Aretha Franklin, David Bowie, and other stars of the hippie rock era.

In the mid-1970s, the appearance of *disco* and *punk* as opposing styles made it clear that the counter-culture experiment with musical art was over. Initially associated with the gay subculture of New York City, disco soon attracted a large teen following. Although despised by many to this day as superficial schlock music, disco had a substantial impact on pop culture, especially after the release of the motion picture *Saturday Night Fever* (1977) and its hugely successful disco soundtrack featuring the Bee Gees. Punk rock stood in stark contrast to disco. It originated around 1976 in London and parts of New York as a reaction against the commercialism of disco and the 'artistic pretentiousness' of counter-culture rock. The precursors to punk rock were 1960s 'surf' rock bands and 'garage' bands such as the Standells and the Seeds. Punk rock was coarse, shrill, and offensive. Early punk groups included the Sex Pistols, the Clash, and the Ramones. A variant, more broadly acceptable form of punk music, *new wave* – as represented, for instance, by Elvis Costello and the Jam – was not, in my mind, that much different. Alienating themselves visibly from mainstream culture, the followers of punk music and new wave emerged as a more menacing threat to the social order than the one posed by their hippie predecessors. The 'Devil's music' seemed to have become de facto satanic. The stage performances of punk musicians were deliberately brutal and conflictual. They mutilated themselves with knives, damaged the props on stage and in the hall, shouted, burped, spat, urinated, and bellowed at will to a basic, rhythmic, pulsating beat, inciting their fans to follow suit. The fashion trends they introduced, as we saw in the second chapter, emphasized degradation, mockery, social caricature, and insubordination at once. Punk teens rejected disco culture with the expression 'disco sucks,' seeing it as too superficial and much too acceptable to the adult world. Theirs was an art of *bricolage*, as culture theorists call it – a process by which elements are appropriated from the dominant culture and their meaning transformed through ironic juxtapositions to challenge and subvert that culture.

But nothing lasts forever in our neomaniacal and forever young culture, where rapid renewal is the only operative principle. By the late 1970s, both disco and punk vanished from the pop-music radar screen, although snippets of the musical forms they introduced have remained to this day. Among the new trends, one of the most popular favoured make-up, cross-dressing, and an overall blurring of the lines between the sexes. The hard-rock band Kiss, whose performances on stage were designed to shock adults, symbolized this new trend perfectly. Each musician assumed a mock comic-book role – a glamour boy, an alien from outer space, a kitty cat, and a sex-crazed Kabuki monster. Band members wore make-up and their stage act included fire eating, smoke bombs, hydraulic lifts, and the smashing of instruments. Two other performers – Michael Jackson and Madonna – challenged traditional gender models even more than Kiss. Madonna's songs 'Like a Virgin,' 'Material Girl,' and 'Dress You Up' blatantly portrayed femininity as objectified sexuality. These topped the hit-parade charts, to the chagrin and dismay of leading feminists of the day. Madonna openly defied the political correctness of the era by adopting a Marilyn Monroe 'sex-kitten' peep-show pose as her performance trademark. Michael Jackson assumed both male and female sexual characteristics for his stage persona. He achieved this through extensive cosmetic surgery. Rock and roll had become, clearly, spectacle, exhibition, and voyeurism packed into one. Shock had become schlock. But it was fun. That's why it caught on with teen audiences.

MTV was launched in 1981 with the video 'Video Killed the Radio Star,' by the Buggles, merging recorded music and television once and for all. The early music videos were hardly the work of artists; they were meant simply to shock – the gorier and more gruesome, the better. MTV was the healthy offspring of the 'TV–rock marriage' – one of the most successful economic marriages of business history. The whole rock-and-roll craze was, in effect, spread throughout society (and the global village) by The Ed Sullivan Show after it hosted Elvis Presley and early rock stars on Sunday evenings in the mid-1950s. The same program catapulted the Beatles to global fame in 1964. An estimated 73 million people watched the show. The moments that link television with the diffusion and promotion of pop music are now part of pop-culture history. In addition to the Elvis Presley and Beatle TV debuts, various other TV events helped to entrench rock as mainstream music rather than just music for adolescents. In 1968, for instance, Elvis Presley made a comeback with his special on NBC, entrenching an 'Elvis subculture' after his death in 1977. Indeed, it is difficult to explain the lasting power of Elvis Presley over subsequent generations ever since that performance, other than to suggest that it is evidence of the power of the TV–rock combination. In 2002, the remix of his song 'A Little Less Conversation,' spliced with techno sounds and electronic warps and woofs – a minor song from 1968, and used on the soundtrack for the even more minor film *Live a Little, Love a Little* – made its way to the top of the charts. All that can be said is that Elvis has become a *sui generis* mythology – a poor country boy who made good and became an international symbol. More to the point, for this book, his memory continues to fuel a passionate denial of aging and extinction. His home, known as Graceland, has become a sacred place, a sprawling fortress that witnessed the final days of a pop-culture icon. He is now an ageless hero. To wit: his songs were featured recently in the hit movie for children *Lilo and Stitch* (Disney, 2002).

After Elvis's comeback performance, television and rock merged texts completely. In 1975, *Saturday Night Live* introduced rock musical acts into its programs, spreading rock music more and more into the mainstream. In 1984, Madonna shocked everyone by appearing in a wedding gown singing 'Like a Virgin' on the MTV Video Awards, emphasizing that rock music and pop-culture trends had become one and the same thing. In 1985, the Live Aid concert was aired by ABC and MTV, rekindling interest in rock as a vehicle for political and social change. In the early 1990s, MTV started its own 'reality TV' program, called *Real World*. The program depicted the lives, loves, and personal traumas confronting the 'MTV generation.' A 1998 poll showed that it was first among basic cable offerings for viewers from twelve to thirty-four years of age in that year.

The TV–rock combination is the stuff of great spectacle, appealing to the eye and the ear at once. In the 1990s, this merger became even more a matter of spectacle and image, as hip-hop musicians, girl-power music groups (such as the Spice Girls and subsequent clone groups), and Latino artists vied for TV air time. Fan loyalties were also split among artists of previous eras and those who represented a new type of crooning music such as Celine Dion and Elton John. Moreover, pop music faced a new source of competition for the music dollar – a renewed interest in classical music and opera brought about mainly by the use of such music by movies of that era. Today, opera probably has as many fans as does any genre of rock. Such is the nature of aesthetics in the ambivalent domain of pop culture!

The powerful role that spectacle has played (and continues to play) in promoting and sustaining the popularity of pop music was highlighted by a *Spin* magazine (5 June 2001) survey of the ten most influential rock performances, artists, or promoters from the 1950s to the year 2000:

1 Lollapalooza, various artists (1991–7)
2 Raising Hell, various artists (1986)
3 The Beatles' U.S. tour (1965)
4 Madonna, The Virgin tour (1985)
5 The Grateful Dead's 'concert tours' (1967–85)
6 Alan Freed's rock 'n' roll package tours (1952–8)
7 Ozzfest, various artists (1998)
8 James Brown's stage performances (1968)
9 Black Flag (1981–2)
10 Up in Smoke tour, various artists (2000)

But spectacles are effective only in an ephemeral way. Like the music played at rock concerts, they tend to evanesce quickly from communal memory. Even the great songs of rock history tend to become *passé* rapidly. The reason is because they refer, ultimately, to an age-specific world of experiences – the adolescent one, as the titles below show. Published in *USA Today* (20 November 2000), these are considered by MTV and *Rolling Stone* magazine to be the all-time greatest rock songs:

1 'Yesterday' – The Beatles
2 '(I Can't Get No) Satisfaction' – The Rolling Stones
3 'Smells Like Teen Spirit' – Nirvana
4 'Like a Virgin' – Madonna
5 'Billie Jean' – Michael Jackson
6 'I Want to Hold Your Hand' – The Beatles
7 'Respect' – Aretha Franklin
8 'One' – U2
9 'I Want You Back' – The Jackson 5
10 'I Want It That Way' – Backstreet Boys

The theme of romance and sex, which is a powerful one in the lives of all teenagers, is mirrored in a straightforward manner in 'I Want to

Hold Your Hand' and 'I Want You Back.' In 'Like a Virgin' and 'Billie Jean' this theme is given a different twist. Madonna's song is a parody of the role played by female teens in sexual relations; Michael Jackson's song reflects instead an explicitness and openness in sexual matters that was unusual for the era in which it was recorded. The rebellious need to assert oneself as different from the existing social order and to inject a new voice into the adult culture through protest is reflected, to varying degrees, in 'Satisfaction,' 'Smells Like Teen Spirit,' 'I Want It That Way,' 'Respect,' and 'One.' The exception is the truly remarkable song 'Yesterday,' which shows to this day how sophisticated pop music can be as a modern form of musical art. Through its wistful melody and philosophical lyrics, the song tells of how fleeting things are in life in ways that parallel the great music of the classical composers. No wonder it was quickly adopted by leading symphony orchestras into their repertoire.

Hip Is Cool

Of all the trends of the 1990s, the one that gained the largest following among teenage audiences was hip-hop music, which traces its roots to the mid-1970s reggae and rap-music styles. The superstar of the reggae style was Bob Marley, who, by the time of his death in 1981, had become one of the most popular musicians in the world. During the 1980s, rap music made its way to the centre of the pop-music entertainment stage. Rock superstars such as Peter Gabriel, David Byrne, and Paul Simon, whose 1985 album *Graceland* featured musicians from Africa and Latin America, played an important role in bringing this about by exposing the works of African-American musicians to audiences in the United States and Europe. Rap is a genre in which vocalists perform rhythmic speech, usually accompanied by music snippets, called *samples*, from pre-recorded material or from music created by synthesizers. The first rap records were made in 1979 by small, independent record companies. Although artists such as the Sugar Hill Gang had national hits during the early 1980s, rap music did not enter the pop-music mainstream until 1986, when rappers Run-D.M.C. and the hard-rock band Aerosmith collaborated on a version of the song 'Walk This Way,' creating a new audience for rap among white, suburban, middle-class rock fans. By the end of the 1980s, MTV had established a program dedicated solely to rap. This made it possible for artists such as M.C. Hammer and the Beastie Boys to achieve enormous success.

The term *rap* is often used interchangeably with *hip-hop*. But the latter was derived from a phrase used in the rap recording 'Rapper's Delight' (1979) by the Sugar Hill Gang. The term *hop*, actually, has been around a long time to describe virtually the same kind of movements as those involved in hip-hop dancing. For example, there is the Lindy hop style originating in Harlem in the 1920s, which is probably better known in its so-called jitterbug version. It was characterized by energetic body rhythms and the improvisational moves of the dancers. The dancers created a heightened energy level and excitement by performing daring aerial movements. The hop dance of early rock and roll, too, was a high-energy acrobatic form of dance. The most famous example of this style was the dance performed to Danny and the Juniors' 1958 hit 'At the Hop.' *Hop* was replaced by *hip* in the 1960s, becoming a code word for the counter-culture views of the 'hippies.' Swinging the hip in a tantalizing way has, of course, sexual overtones. It is *the* basic movement in belly-dancing and striptease. But the hippies used it to convey a new, brash, anti-establishment attitude. It is little wonder, therefore, that the style of music known as hip-hop is a combination of both terms. It is music that involves sexual dancing at the same time that it conveys subversive messages. What could be more *cool*?

The rise of rap and hip-hop in many ways parallels the birth of rock and roll in the 1950s. Both originated within the African-American culture, and both were initially recorded by small, independent record labels and marketed almost exclusively to black audiences. In both cases, the new style gradually attracted white musicians, a few of whom began performing it. For rock and roll it was a white American from Mississippi, Elvis Presley, who broke into the *Billboard* magazine popular-music charts. For rap it was a white group from New York City, the Beastie Boys. Their release of '(You Gotta) Fight for Your Right (to Party)' (1986) was one of the first two rap records to reach the *Billboard* top-ten list of popular hits. The other was, as mentioned, 'Walk This Way' (1986). Soon after 1986, the use of samples and quasi-spoken vocal styles became widespread in the popular music of both black and white performers, significantly altering previous notions of what constitutes a legitimate song, composition, or musical accompaniment.

Hip-hop music typically emphasizes lyrics and wordplay over melody and harmony, achieving interest through rhythmic complexity and variations in the timing of the lyrics. Hip-hop is not unlike the popular musical form developed in Italy in the late thirteenth and early fourteenth centuries known as the madrigal – an unaccompanied vocal composition for two or three voices in simple harmony, following a strict poetic form. Hip-hop was, in my view, the madrigal music of the 1990s. Its lyric themes can be broadly categorized under three rubrics: (1) those that concern human relationships; (2) those chronicling and embracing the so-called gangsta lifestyle of youths who live in inner cities; and (3) those addressing contemporary aspects of the black experience. But in the pop-music business, ephemerality is the first law of the marketplace. The hip-hopper's acerbic indictments of society have now become mere formulas in a new grammar of cool. Even in its so-called gangsta form, which depicts an outlaw lifestyle of sex, drugs, and violence in inner-city America, hip-hop has come to be perceived as a vehicle to express coolness, not subversion. Incidentally, the first major album of gangsta rap, *Straight Outta Compton*, was released in 1988 by the rap group N.W.A. (Niggaz With Attitude). Songs from the album generated an extraordinary amount of controversy on account of their violent messages. The album provoked protests from a number of organizations, including the FBI. However, attempts to censor gangsta rap only served to publicize the music and make it more attractive to youths generally. As Robert R. Provine remarks in his insightful work on cultural texts, 'Like it or not, rap works, and is one of the significant developments in music and poetry in recent decades. Rap lyrics gain priority access to the emotional centres of the brain – they kick in the doors of our auditory attention centres and demand to be heard.'[4]

Hip-hop culture introduced the practice of using nicknames, known as *tags*, as part of a new form of tribalism among teens. For a few years, these were commonly etched on the urban landscape – on bus shelters, buses, subways, signs, walls, freeway overpasses, mailboxes, and so on – with markers, spray paint, or shoe polish (*Futura 2000*, *Phase 2*, *Zephyr*, *Crash*). In this way, hip-hop teens advertised their new identity to everyone. To symbolize the event, the tag was decorated with crowns, stars, arrows, underlines, halos, and so on. There were two main forms of decoration – *throw-ups* and *pieces*. The former consisted in spray-painting one's new name in bubble, block, or some other expansive style; the latter in decorating it with characters from cartoons or with proverbs. In such cities as Los Angeles and New York, hip-hop teens made thousands of murals.

So interesting had hip-hop tagging art become by the late 1990s that some traditional art galleries even started putting it on display. In

December of 2000, the Brooklyn Museum of Art organized an exposition of 400 pieces of urban street art, called *Hip-Hop Nation: Roots, Rhymes and Rage*, reflecting more than three decades of hip-hop art. In a city where nearly 2000 arrests for graffiti offences were carried out in the same year, the art gallery had taken on the role previously confined to the streets.

Much like the hippies of the 1960s, or the punks of the 1970s, teens who became involved in hip-hop culture in the 1990s did so primarily to assert independence from their families. Paradoxically, what made such involvement attractive to youths was the promise of a highly organized family-like social structure. Did it mean that their families did not provide such structure? Or, did it mean that the family had become so devalued as an institution that it was viewed as useless by the teens? I will return to this topic in the next chapter. Suffice it to say here that such pseudo-family enclaves as those that characterized the hippie communes of the 1960s or the hip-hop tribes of the 1990s provide the authority structure that families seem to lack. The hip-hop world is, indeed, systematized into classes, subgroups (networks of friends), and mentor–protégé relationships. Joining a hip-hop clique entails taking on a tag nickname, which is often determined by peers – a ritual acknowledging that one is noticed, included, and individualized. Such names have unusual emotional power. Putting one's nickname on a surface is a form of public statement. It announces to the world that the individual is reborn with an identity of his or her own making. As one interviewee told me, 'to be all-city [to have one's name appearing in many different places and areas] is what every hip-hop person is out to do.'

As part of 'identity construction,' rap artists and hip-hop teens spell their names in ways that imitate 'street Black English.' No doubt this is intended to communicate to the mainstream that rappers belong to a culture that sets itself apart from the mainstream. For this reason, they will spell the English language on their own terms – *boyz* instead of *boys*, *dogg* instead of *dog*, and so on. But again, there is nothing new in such teen trends. The hippies in the 1960s intentionally called themselves *freeks* and considered the spelling *Amerika* to be a political statement.

For a brief period of time in the 1990s, heavy metal and rap joined forces to produce so-called *rap-metal* music. The style was directed primarily at macho male types known as *mooks*. Its message was a combination of rage, profanity, and blatant sexuality. Groups such as Korn and Limp Bizkit, as well as the controversial artist Eminem, symbolized this new trend. Along with the music of gangsta rappers such as Ice-T, Dr. Dre, and Snoop Doggy Dogg, rap-metal music became particularly worrisome to parents, who fretted especially over the brutal and hard-core sexual lyrics of the music. At the start of the year 2000, female rap-metal bands also came into the spotlight, showing as much rage and profanity as their male counterparts, adding to the uneasiness felt by many adults about the music. As I write, this movement has dissipated, and even previously popular groups such as Limp Bizkit have declined in popularity and may even have disappeared from the pop-culture radar screen by the time this book comes out.

Why all the rage? Was it (is it) a legitimate response to the shallowness and corruption of a consumer-crazed world? Was it (is it) a way to let off steam, much safer than walking through a high school corridor with a weapon under one's coat? Was it (is it) rage against family break-ups and divorce? Maybe. But, by and large, in my view the rage bands were nothing more than products of media moguls, who had discovered already in the counter-culture era how to co-opt the music of rebellion, transforming it into worthless pap. The mook musicians and their fans were (are) hardly individuals caught in an underclass situation, or teens who felt (feel) oppressed and victimized. Rather, like the 'rebels without a cause' of the 1950s, they were (are) primarily bored, middle-class youths who espouse rage music as a veiled attempt to eschew the responsibilities of growing up. The many teens interviewed by the research team on this topic were quick to point out that mooks are mainly 'fakes,' as one fifteen-year-old labelled them. Most of the interviewees hardly perceived the fascination with rage music as legitimately arising from individuals caught in a socially desperate situation. Rather, they perceived it as the expression of rage for its own sake, as 'a trick to be bratty kids again,' as one interviewee sagaciously put it; 'it's a way of being lazy and nothing more,' she continued. This is perhaps why all the rage gets channelled fairly quickly into marketable niches where it can be appreciated without any undue impact on the larger society.

As I write, I sense a decrease in the hegemony that rage and hip-hop culture have had in the adolescent realm. Several violent deaths in rap, especially those of Tupac Shakur, Notorious B.I.G., and Jam Master Jay (of the group Run-D.M.C.), may be signs of a larger malaise in rap culture, a world marked by insults, gang mentality, taunts, menaces, and blood feuds. But, then, these may be nothing but the ultimate 'come-ons' for a music industry that is still thriving at the start of the twenty-first century with several billions of dollars, but on the verge of losing its grip and, ultimately, ending up like every other previous music industry – in the background. The signs of this are unmistakable. Many rappers now taunt each other in their songs and on television directly, rather than decrying social inequalities. No wonder, then, that a *New York Times* 2002 survey found that most of the top rap artists at the time were 'historical figures' in the rap movement – Dr. Dre, Warren G, Puff Daddy, Eminem, Shaggy, Ja Rule, SMX, Nelly, Ludacris, Coolio, Salt-N-Pepa, and Snoop Doggy Dogg. Only a couple were still in their twenties at the time.[5] Further evidence of rap's demise comes from a 2002 *Rolling Stone* poll that asked its readers to choose their 100 all-time favourite albums. The top ten chosen were as follows:

1 *Revolver*, The Beatles (1965)
2 *Nevermind*, Nirvana (1991)
3 *Sgt. Pepper's Lonely Hearts Club Band*, The Beatles (1967)
4 *The Joshua Tree*, U2 (1987)
5 *The White Album*, The Beatles (1968)
6 *Abbey Road*, The Beatles (1969)
7 *Appetite for Destruction*, Guns n' Roses (1987)
8 *OK Computer*, Radiohead (1997)
9 *Led Zeppelin*, Led Zeppelin (1971)
10 *Achtung Baby*, U2 (1991)

Surveys such as this show that rap is starting to be considered, by and large, a marginal art form by the current consumers of pop music – no matter what music critics and academics say. It is beginning to appeal less and less to the audiences that matter – the newer generations of teenagers.

As a final word on the topic of rap, I cannot but mention the phenomenon of the 'white rapper' Eminem. In 2002, he eclipsed even the African-American rapper Ja Rule. In his widely acclaimed movie, *8 Mile*, Eminem was raised to the level of a pseudo-mythology. The movie got its name from an east–west road in Detroit that once divided city from suburb, blacks from whites, lower class from middle class. The movie, directed by Curtis Hanson, was essentially a semi-biographical drama featuring suburbia's angriest white rapper, Eminem. It recreated 1995 Detroit when the hip-hop movement was at its peak. Its goal was, to my mind, simply to carve Eminem into a new Elvis Presley in rap clothing – a white man making a black man's art his own. Once denounced as a threat to America's moral fibre, he was transformed by the movie into an 'acceptable' icon of pop music. His shows subsequently started to draw little kids and their parents! His music was acclaimed by music critics as the stuff of great irony and iconoclasm combined. But I fail to hear it. And even if it is there, in whatever form, there is still more irony and iconoclastic power built into a Beethoven bagatelle lasting less than a minute than there is in Eminem's total musical output.

Grooving On

As I write, change is again taking place all over the pop-music universe. So-called *techno* groups, who combine computer-generated, discolike rhythms with digital sounds, and *acid jazz* bands, who combine rock, soul, rhythm-and-blues, and jazz influences into an eclectic style, became somewhat popular at the millennium. But they were quickly thrust into competition with artists representing a plethora of new and recycled music styles. The only 'constant' in pop music, alas, is that of 'constant change.'

Sexuality still dominates pop-music lyrics. And, as in the hippie 1960s, protest and a general critique of society are found in many songs. Groups such as Rage Against the Machine are promoted as purportedly continuing the tradition of Dylan and Crosby, Stills, Nash, and Young of expressing rage against the 'system.' For some reason, since the 1960s some rock musicians feel impelled to constantly rant and scream against anything that exists in society. But although such music appears to have a transgressive or subversive intent, like all other things in modern society it ends up being nothing more than the shrieking of a pampered group of self-anointed pseudo-activists whose ultimate goal is to get teens to buy their CDs and music videos.

Why does such strident pap, along with other kinds of slop, continue to attract audiences? It seems that, in our forever young culture, there is an unwritten law that the rocking, swinging, grooving, and ranting must go on *ad infinitum*. The paradox of modern pop culture is, in fact, that art and pap get mixed up and often mistaken for each other. The work of genuine artists is thrown into the barrel along with that of mere entertainers. Even hip-hop music, as interesting as it is, rarely rises above the voices of the hip and cool. It now seems to be more about gold rings, gold chains, sex, and brand-name sneakers than about social protest. The hip-hop subculture, like the hippie and punk subcultures before it, started out as genuine rebellion. But the instant the music and fashions were adopted by the mainstream culture, the rebellion faded and economics took over.

Every musical style has, of course, a life cycle. Baroque music survived as the dominant style from about 1650 to 1750; the classical forms of Haydn and Mozart persisted from the 1770s to well into the nineteenth century, when Beethoven and other composers radically altered them to bring about the so-called romantic movement; and serious composers in the twentieth century, from Bartok and Stravinsky to Shostakovich and Prokofiev, constantly experimented with new ways to make profound music. But pop music has shown itself to be particularly inclined to change rapidly and to pass from communal memory. Its ephemerality or 'short life' is, no doubt, a reflection of the pop culture it mirrors. As emotionally powerful as any given pop-music genre is to a particular group of people, it quickly loses its sway over subsequent generations. The music of Bach, Mozart, Beethoven, Bartok, and Prokofiev, on the other hand, does not.

In a recent book titled *If It Ain't Got That Swing*, Mark Gavreau Judge argues that Chuck Berry's 1955 hit song 'Roll Over Beethoven' signalled the end of 'adult forms' of music.[6] As a consequence, it also heralded the demise of adult culture, bringing on a full-fledged teen-aging of music, fashion, and life. I agree. Berry's choice of Beethoven as the symbol of 'adult music' was, in hindsight, a total misconception. In the title and lyrics of his song, Berry was alluding to the snobbery and élitism that classical music aficionados tend to show with regard to other kinds of musical tastes. By extension, his song was meant to assert the right of adolescents to enjoy their own kind of music, a music that expressed a new freedom – a liberation from the strictures of society. But Berry obviously did not understand that his choice of composers was a truly infelicitous one. In actual fact, there is nothing more liberating, passionate, and truly subversive than Beethoven's music. Never, absolutely never, has rock been able to come close to expressing the kind of fury and rage that can be heard in his *Appassionata* sonata, or the profound spirituality that imbues his *Missa Solemnis*.

In many ways, Beethoven has been 'rolled over,' as Berry predicted. Rock musicians organize charity concerts in aid of worldwide causes. And in the weeks following the 11 September tragedy, the paragons of pop music came out in full force, offering up their musical elegies in order to give melodic expression to communal grief. Music has always played a central role in collective grieving. The great requiem masses of Mozart and Verdi, for example, provided a powerful channel for communal grief to be expressed in the open. They put sound to sorrow, despair, and anguish. Their music transformed and continues to transform all those who listen to it. To the best of my recollection, the last time classical music was used in communal grieving was during the funerary ceremonies for President John F. Kennedy in 1963. Throughout the solemn ceremonies, shown on television, one could hear the powerfully moving second-movement 'funeral march' of Beethoven's *Eroica* symphony. Kennedy's status in history as a tragic hero was thus guaranteed. Significantly, Kennedy's death was memorialized with Beethoven, Princess Diana's with Elton John.

The big experiment to transform rock into musical art – a movement that can perhaps be characterized as 'joining up with Beethoven,' in contrast to 'rolling over Beethoven' – started, of course, in the counter-culture era. To this day, music critics can be heard raving about the music they obviously loved and grew up with. And, indeed, it was a wonderful experiment. Some of the musicians of the era were truly outstanding poets and composers. The group known as Procol Harum is a case in point. Their 'Salty Dog' and 'A Whiter Shade of Pale' are classifiable as true works of musical art. But a closer look at their music reveals that it is 'classical music with a rock beat to it,' as one teen informant recently characterized it to me after listening to it on my request. Revealingly, although he liked the music very much, and was intent on becoming more familiar with it, he also concluded to me as follows: 'As good as it is, I might as well listen to Bach or Mozart.'

As the teen's words prophetically imply, the experiment seems to have faded, except for those die-hard rock aficionados of the 1960s, becoming increasingly an object of nostalgia. In 1995, the Rock and Roll Hall of Fame opened in Cleveland, Ohio – a sure sign that rock had become 'museum music.' Also in the 1990s, several major television documentaries were produced on the history of rock and roll, and historical box-set recordings were reissued featuring rock artists from the past – further signs that rock music had become more a part of history than of current interest. Today, 'oldies' radio stations have as large a following as those promoting contemporary music, if not larger. As rock musician David Byrne (1952–) has put it, 'As I define it, rock &

roll is dead. The attitude isn't dead, but the music is no longer vital. It doesn't have the same meaning.'[7]

On the other hand, Beethoven's music is not dead; nor will it ever die. Beethoven simply cannot be 'rolled over.' The reader must not misunderstand me. I myself was a jazz and rock musician and totally enjoyed playing such music. I still do. But ultimately I have to admit, to myself at the very least, that it does not ennoble the human condition, certainly not in the same way that, say, Rossini's *Stabat Mater* or Mozart's *Requiem* do. Those works are timeless and ageless. Pop music is 'time-bound,' becoming quickly 'aged.'[8] As the French-born American critic and novelist George Steiner (1929–) stated in 1971, rock and roll is appealing 'for the moment' because it has come to constitute the universal language of teens in the global village, cutting 'across languages, ideologies, frontiers and races.'[9] There is no denying the influence of such music on teens. It breeds concentric worlds of fashion, language, lifestyle, and world-view. As Roberts and Christenson[10] and Holloway,[11] among many other cultural observers, have aptly observed, pop music has always played, and will probably continue to play, a central role in the life of adolescents, as long as adolescence is around.

But what do pop songs have to say to one and all? They deal with juvenile themes and are performed by juvenile artists – artists, incidentally, who try to hang on to their youth with an alarming degree of desperation. Cher and Michael Jackson, for instance, were continually undergoing cosmetic surgery in the 1990s in order to maintain a pseudo-adolescent appearance. Cher finally decided to throw in the towel in 2002, declaring her retirement from the stage. It was, however, only a few years before that, in 1998, that she made an album for the young audiences of the time, *Believe*, that sold more than 10 million copies worldwide. The similarly named single became her biggest hit ever. But it was irritating to see Cher always experimenting, in the same period, with new kinds of music styles, from metallic to hip-hop, in order to maintain her place in the spotlight. And what can one say about Michael Jackson? Since around 2001 he has been dressing as ghoulishly as he was in his *Thriller* video, constantly shaping his public persona through bizarre facial cosmetics.

Even rap and hip-hop musicians have been afflicted by the FYS. Many older rappers now show up in movies and TV programs, dressed up and acting as they did years before when their music meant something. And then, of course, there are the Rolling Stones, those ageless rockers who, at the start of the twenty-first century, are still rock-ing away. As Stephen Davis has recently called them, they are 'old gods almost dead.'[12] In 2002, the Stones went on a tour, called Licks, to sold-out audiences wherever they played.

I suppose, once a rock and roller always a rock and roller. Inciden-tally, Mick Jagger, the lead singer of the Stones, received a British knighthood in 2002 at the age of fifty-eight – an event that could mate-rialize only in a forever young world, given that Mick Jagger was, in his heyday, the epitome of subversion. But, as I witnessed at the 1994 Grateful Dead concert I attended (see chapter 1), the performances of old gods are profoundly sad. They are performances by old people pathetically reconstituting their adolescent selves. No wonder that new generations of teens are continually trying to keep one step ahead. Someone simply has to tell our 'rock and roll gods,' as Davis calls them, that it is time to fade away, like many of their classic songs. And someone should tell the TV executives that the time has also come to put to rest the constant praise of veteran pop musicians. Specials of Bruce Springsteen, Garth Brooks, Madonna, and others, designed to keep the mythology of rock and pop music alive, are constantly being shown on specialty channels. But who is watching? And, more impor-tantly, who really cares? As John Strausbaugh has argued, rock has long outlived its function.[13]

Aside from a few cases (such as the Cher example mentioned above), the newer generations of teens rarely show interest in music legends from previous generations. They are 'dead brands,' as one informant put it to me. The 'fade-out' of the icons of pop culture is inevitable, for pop culture is designed to be ephemeral. Janis Joplin has given way to Britney Spears who will give way to whoever the 'latest female icon' is as this book goes to press – all the reader has to do is fill in the blanks. The 2000 CD of the Beatles' greatest hits was successful because the teen generation of that year simply bought it as a gift to their parents. Less than half of 1 per cent of people aged eight to twenty-four years old named the Beatles in that year as their favourite performers, according to a 2001 Zandl survey. Similar percentages were registered for Bob Marley and Jimi Hendrix. Dead icons resonate mainly with the generation that knew them as performers.

The chances are that, as this book goes to press, the hip-hop move-ment will have given way to something completely different. The con-stant change in teen music and lifestyle trends is now a fact of everyday life. The entire economic system in which we live seems to have become completely dependent upon an incessant craving for the *new* – *new music, new fashion, new everything*. The paradox of modern culture today is that it is both inclined to change rapidly and yet highly predictable in the way it changes. Having said all this, I believe that a true shift in musical sophistication among the young themselves may have started to take shape. Many adolescents are taking more and more of a genuine interest in classical music. Bored with the constant-craze mentality of new musical fads, new musical icons, and simply bad music, scores of teens have told me in interviews that the music of Mozart or Beethoven is something 'exciting and new' for them.

If music is so influential in shaping character, then is it not advisable to expose children, from birth, to the suggestive power of great music – from Bach and Mozart to the works of Prokofiev and Glass? As children become adolescents, this early formation will not go away, no matter how much they might experiment with cool and faddish musical styles. As Greil Marcus put it in 1976, in the end, 'Rock 'n' roll is a combination of good ideas dried up by fads, terrible junk, hideous failings in taste and judgment, gullibility and manipulation, moments of unbelievable clarity and invention, pleasure, fun, vulgarity, excess, novelty and utter enervation.'[14]

Musicologists believe, by and large, that music originally had a ritualistic and mythological function. The notion of musicians as individualists and eccentric creators is a modern one. In ancient cultures, music was meant to be used in ceremonies. It was made by various members of the community rather than by professional artists alone. In traditional aboriginal cultures of North America, in fact, music and dance continue to be perceived as aspects of community rituals that are designed to ensure a good harvest or to celebrate a significant life event such as a birth or a marriage. But even in modern Western cultures, music continues to reverberate with ritualistic overtones. At a performance of a classical piece of music in a concert hall, for instance, there is ritualistic silence. At a rock concert, on the other hand, there is communal shouting and physical involvement.

The ancient philosophers of classical Greece believed that music originated with Apollo and Orpheus, and that it reflected in its melodic and harmonic structure the laws of harmony that rule the universe. They also believed that music influences human thoughts and actions, because each melody possesses an emotional quality that listeners experience directly. Opinions differ about such 'emotional theories' of music, and about what I have called the transformative or spiritual value of music. But throughout the world there seems to be an implicit understanding that music is one of the most powerful of the arts that we employ to express our inner nature. In some African societies, for instance, music is considered to be the faculty that sets humans apart from other species; among some Native Americans, it is thought to have originated as a way for spirits to communicate with human beings.

The question of what constitutes musical art is not an easy one to answer, because art appeals to our feelings more than it does to our intellect. But one thing is certain – only those works that are genuinely meaningful to one and all will remain. Beethoven's *Missa Solemnis* and his last four string quartets, to mention but two examples, will remain because they convey, through sound, a profound inner quest for meaning in life. Rummaging through the pop-music experiment of the last fifty years will not, in my view, produce anything that comes even close to the Beethovenian standard.

All this might sound élitist to the reader. But it is not. In his great operas *Le nozze di Figaro* and *Die Zauberflöte*, Mozart wrote music that he intended for the enjoyment of common folk – not just the cognoscenti. This is true as well of all of nineteenth-century Italian operas. The operas of Verdi and Rossini were 'populist' events. The idea of 'classical music' as an élitist form of art is a modern idea. And it is a myth that simply needs to be dispelled, once and for all. We are lucky to live in an era where the music of Mozart or Beethoven need not lie dormant. It can be heard for the price of a CD. Their music 'does us good,' as the Swiss philosopher and poet Henri-Frédéric Amiel (1821–81) wrote a century and a half ago:[15]

> Mozart has the classic purity of light and the blue ocean; Beethoven the romantic grandeur which belongs to the storms of air and sea, and while the soul of Mozart seems to dwell on the ethereal peaks of Olympus, that of Beethoven climbs shuddering the storm-beaten sides of a Sinai. Blessed be they both! Each represents a moment of the ideal life, each does us good. Our love is due to both.

The music of Mozart and Beethoven cannot be easily managed by the entrepreneurs of taste. It will exist regardless of the economic system in place in a future society. As a final word on the topic of music, it is ironic to reflect on the fact that the greatest composers of all time were barely 'teenagers' when they composed some of their greatest works. And they died at ages that today would be considered way too young. To wit: Mozart died at the age of thirty-five, Chopin at thirty-nine, and Schubert at thirty-one. But their music was and continues to be 'ageless' and 'timeless.'

CHAPTER FIVE

Time to Grow Up

Above all, though, children are linked to adults by the simple fact that they are in process of turning into them. For this they may be forgiven much. Children are bound to be inferior to adults, or there is no incentive to grow up.

Philip Larkin (1922–1985)

In *The Catcher in the Rye*, Holden Caulfield wanted to stop children from growing up and entering the world of adolescence and adulthood – a world that he found to be contaminated by hypocrisy, shallowness, and bigotry. Caulfield is a modern-day descendant of Goethe's Werther. He is the romantic hero who sees childhood as the only period of life uncontaminated by the hypocrisy that marks human social relations. And, like nineteenth-century romantic heroes, Caulfield is guided by a fragmentary form of consciousness that produces his momentary flashes of inspiration and insight – what the poet Percy Bysshe Shelley (1792–1822) called 'enchanted chords.' Ironically and absurdly, it is the same kind of fragmentary consciousness that fuels the engines of the whole distraction factory in which we live. As the great writer Hermann Hesse (1877–1962) remarked in his last novel, *Magister Ludi* (1949), we live in an age that reduces everything to digestible fragments.[1] It is an age, consequently, that has fostered an obsessive need within us for information and objects *for their own sake*. This is the reason why television is vastly more popular than reading. The amount of fragmentary information presented in a short period of time on a news program, for instance, is torrential. We are able to take it all in because it is edited and stylized for effortless mass consumption. The camera moves in to select aspects of a situation – to show a face that cares, that is suffering, that is happy, that is angry – and then shifts to the cool, handsome face of an anchorman or to the attractive one of an anchorwoman to tell us what it's all about. The news items, the film footage, the commentaries are all fast-paced and brief. They are designed to be visually dramatic fragments of easily digestible information.

In his poetic novel *Siddhartha* (1922), Hesse showed that the way to reintegrate the fragments of our consciousness into a spiritual whole is actually rather straightforward. In the novel, Siddhartha (the young Buddha) sought wisdom and spiritual wholeness by moving away from the fragmentary world in which he lived so that he could take the necessary time to reflect upon things holistically and at length. That is the powerful message that Hesse's novel holds for us today – we must take more time to reflect on things, ignoring for the most part the fragmentary images of life that the media constantly promulgate. As social critic Todd Gitlin has aptly put it, the media perpetrate a relentless barrage of sensation, instant transition, and non-stop stimuli.[2] They fuel celebrity cults, paranoia, and, above all else, an ironic view of the world. We simply must attempt to reinstate into our groupthink a wholesome, unfragmented view of human experience and human reality.

In this final chapter, I argue that the time has come to seriously consider eliminating our romantic view of adolescence because it has been a primary contributor to the creation of our fragmentary form of consciousness. I will also argue that adolescence has been a key factor in bringing about the FYS.

Eliminating Adolescence

A few years before his death, the American philosopher Eric Hoffer (1902–83) stated bluntly that 'a modern society can remain stable only by eliminating adolescence, by giving its young, from the age of ten, the skills, responsibilities, and rewards of grownups, and opportunities for action in all spheres of life.'[3] Is Hoffer right? Is the elimination of adolescence the only way to get rid of both the so-called traumas of young people and the FYS that continues to plague our culture as a whole? In my view, Hoffer has hit the nail on the head. Hoffer's book, among others (including the present one), constitutes an attempt to raise the awareness of young and old alike to the insanity of continuing with our romantic view of adolescence – a view, incidentally, of which adolescents themselves have become critical (as my interviews suggest).

In the meantime, myths about adolescence, and problems connected with it, persist.[4] The greatest myth of all – and it needs to be dispelled as soon as possible – is that the 'crises' and 'traumas' of adolescence are 'natural' consequences of human development. No such crises were reported in previous centuries, nor are they reported in other societies today. The *Sturm und Drang* view of adolescence is a romantic myth – no more, no less. And, of course, it is a convenient myth for the hordes of 'professionals' who are 'trained' to deal with the problems of adolescence. Rearing children into adulthood is not a science. Reading the relevant literature on childhood development, on the sociology of youth, on juvenile delinquency, and so on, puts one in no better position to provide meaningful insight on growing up than relying on what a mother or a father working on gut instinct alone already knows. When has any social scientist with a scientific or clinical method ever resolved the personal dilemmas of a troubled teen? From my interviews with teens, I am told constantly that, well-meaning though the so-called experts are, they are nevertheless perceived as patronizing because they assume they know what is best for teens. There is no guaranteed 'right' or 'wrong' way to deal with teenagers. Individual cases differ; they cannot possibly be handled systematically or scientifically. As parents of troubled teens know all too well, things simply have to work themselves out. Understanding adolescence in its cultural dimensions is the only true 'source of knowledge' that may help modern-day parents cope with the widely divergent situations they face on a daily basis. The social scientists are, in effect, modern culture's replacements for the shamans and magicians who were once expected to have all the right answers.

The patronizing attitudes of the 'experts' were particularly blatant in the late 1940s and early 1950s, when they made the first classroom sex-education films for adolescents in high school. The titles of these films tell their own story: *Dating: Do's and Don'ts* (1949), *What to Do on a Date* (1951), *More Dates for Kay* (1952), *Age of Turmoil* (1953), and *Social-Sex Attitudes in Adolescence* (1953). With their simple-minded scripts, the films were intended to be doses of 'mental hygiene' for the new hordes of teens, as a retrospective anthology of these films – *Mental Hygiene: Classroom Films, 1945–1970*, by film historian Ken Smith – recently showed (2002). Significantly, they addressed the same kinds of worries that besiege parents today, even if the scripts portrayed teen life in a quaint and rather ludicrous fashion. By the 1960s and 1970s, it became obvious that the approach was infantile. The new films were consequently structured around 'cautionary tales,' which showed teens slaughtered in automobile accidents, suffering from venereal diseases, or ravaged by drug use. But from one generation to the next, nothing really seems to change. Today, all kinds of sophisticated audio-visual materials are used in schools throughout the continent to provide teens with information on sex and dating. It appears that, as the French say, 'plus ça change, plus c'est la même chose' ('The more it changes, the more it is the same'). Rarely have we stopped to consider that this whole line of attack may be misguided, enlightened though it claims to be. A 2002 Planned Parenthood survey found, revealingly, that two-thirds of graduating high school seniors have had some form of sex, one million teens a year get pregnant, and one in four new sexually transmitted diseases occurs in adolescence.

As a teenager myself in the late 1950s and as a parent of a teenager in the early 1980s, I assumed that adolescence was a naturally 'troublesome' adjustment stage of development. But since becoming directly involved with adolescents, both as students and as subjects of research projects, I have come to understand at first hand what the anthropologist Margaret Mead warned about back in the 1930s. There is nothing natural about the problems of adolescence; they have come about because we have interfered with the continuous pattern of growth that individuals would otherwise follow from childhood to adulthood. Few heeded Mead's warning at the time because, already in her era, the *Sturm und Drang* view of adolescence had become an unconscious pattern in our groupthink. At the same time, the business world was starting to eye the potential of adolescence as a marketable commodity. Today, the adolescent market has, in fact, become the single most important cog in the economic machine. It is estimated that teens spend more than $160 billion in North America on everything from sneakers to posters of media stars. A recent Canadian national marketing study found that in the average teen pocket sits $107 of disposable income per week.

Adolescence has been especially good for the discipline of psychology. The numbers of practitioners involved in counselling adolescents, and of books written and sold on the problems of adolescence, have reached worrisome proportions. Psychology has, in effect, declared ownership of adolescence. It is relevant to note that, in 2002, the National Academy of Sciences of the United States decided to define the period of adolescence as stretching from puberty to thirty years of age. In the same year, the McArthur Foundation went one step farther, pegging the end of adolescence at the mind-boggling age of thirty-four! Something is amiss here. How long can we, as a society, allow such views to go unchallenged? In 1970, a group of pediatricians formed the Society for Adolescent Medicine, which became a board-certified branch of pediatrics in 1995. In that year, the society declared that adolescence ended at twenty-six. Seven years later the period has been increased by eight years. Does this mean that, every seven years the age of adolescence will be extended by eight years? I am positive that, in their wildest imaginings, the dramatists of the theatre of the absurd could not have thought up anything more absurd than this. What the profession of psychiatry has ended up doing is nothing short of depriving young people of the right to assert themselves as adults. Psychiatrists have joined forces with economists in promoting a self-serving view of adolescence. This simply must stop. I cannot but agree with the great American writer Henry Miller (1891–1980), who pointed out, disparagingly, that 'In America youth means simply athleticism, disrespect, gangsterism, or sickly idealism expressing itself through thinly disguised and badly digested social science theories acted out by idiots who are desperadoes at heart.'[5] And yet, those desperadoes seem to be gaining more and more empowerment. There is even a movement afoot within psychiatry to require married couples to take courses in child rearing before becoming parents. Spurred on by the many abuse cases that seem to plague the modern family, the promoters of the movement truly believe that there is a rational, scientific approach to bringing up children. But only in our foolish, fragmented age is such an idea even thinkable. In actual fact, most teens prefer to get by in a difficult family situation rather than be sent away to be under the care of others. Only in serious abuse cases has any teen ever expressed to me the desire to leave home, and even then it is with great trepidation and unease.

Eliminating adolescence, thus, entails three obvious things: (1) eliminating our social-scientific view of it; (2) restoring worth to the family as an institution; and (3) imbuing media representations of adolescence and family life with more dignity. Abandoning the view of adolescence as a natural stage of growth is the starting point. The term *adolescens* ('adolescent'), as mentioned in the first chapter, was used as far back as the Middle Ages to refer to any boy, irrespective of age, who began to work independently. But in no sense did it have any of the social connotations that it has today. Ultimately, it comes from the Latin word *adolescere*, meaning 'to grow up,' while the past participle, *adultus*, the source of *adult*, means 'grown up.' The *Oxford English Dictionary* points out that the word *adolescent*, first recorded in English in a work written in 1440, seems to have come into the language before *adult*, which was first recorded in a work published in 1531, implying that the divisive, age-based social categories we carry on our collective shoulders today were certainly not part of groupthink in the past. It was only when Stanley G. Hall put forward a new 'psychological' view of adolescence in 1904 that *adolescentia* took on the meaning that it has today. Unfortunately, Hall's view of adolescence has become a self-fulfilling prophecy. And the constant 'studies' that are continually making it to the *New York Times* best-seller list constitute a true epidemic of psychological bluffing. One such study is Rachel Simmons's *Odd Girl Out: The Hidden Culture of Aggression in Girls*.[6] Although its description of the cruelties females perpetrate on each other in high school is something that I can certainly confirm as verifiable, the 'study's' supercilious approach and moralizing tone – we are not sure who is being scolded, teens, society, or both – makes it nerve-wracking reading. It is in trying to generalize from particular instances that such works go awry, simply capitalizing on parental dread by portraying school as littered with beaten-down adolescents. They are playing to stereotypes – no more, no less.

The second line of attack for eliminating adolescence consists in restoring authority to the family. As psychologist Terri Apter has recently argued, children are slow to become adults because many parents, acting in the name of love, think that children need the time and space to suffer through their own mistakes.[7] But nothing could be farther from the truth. Adolescents need their parents' guidance and support. Guidance is hardly something that they will get from life experiences. Guidance is necessary at all stages of life. Children need guidance; adults do as well. Why do we assume that adolescents do not? Incidentally, a 1999 survey of twelve- to fourteen-year-olds found that 79 per cent identified parents as the people they look up to the most. The next category was athletes, at 13 per cent.[8]

Because of the prolonged stage of brain and skull development in relation to the time required to reach sexual maturity in our species, neonatal human beings are susceptible to unparalleled risks among primates. Each new infant is born with relatively few innate traits yet with a vast number of potential behaviours, and therefore must be reared in a family setting so that it can achieve its potential. It was Freud who started the process of devaluation of this critical institution, claiming that the family was a dysfunctional system, set up as a 'super-ego structure' to impart society's mores to children. He used a very clever argument, bolstered by his so-called case studies, to make his point persuasive. He simply proposed that the psychic problems of adolescents and adults were caused by childhood traumas. The therapeutic procedure he invented involved inducing a hypnotic state in which the patient recalled and re-enacted the traumatic experience, thus discharging by catharsis the emotions causing the symptoms. But the technique never produced the results Freud intended it to produce. So, he turned to the technique of 'free association,' investigating the patient's spontaneous flow of thoughts to reveal, purportedly, the unconscious mental processes at the root of the neurotic disturbance. Freud finally had the evidence he needed to establish the mental mechanisms of *repression*, which he defined as an unconscious set of painful childhood memories operating on the conscious mind, and *resistance*, which he defined as the unconscious defence against awareness of repressed experiences. Freud based his repression theory primarily on his particular interpretation of his patients' dreams and of their slips of the tongue. This led him to claim that infantile sexuality was controlled by a so-called Oedipus complex – the child's erotic attachment to the parent of the opposite sex, with hostile feelings towards the other parent. The Oedipus complex was, Freud declared, the source of most of our problems.

What is amazing to me is that Western society bought Freud's insane ideas *tout court*. His views have, of course, been debated and disputed. However, his general notion that childhood traumas are produced by the family system of rearing, remaining 'latent' throughout life, has not disappeared. But it is simply not true. It took a great writer of fiction, Michael Crichton (1943–), to make this point public for all to grasp. In a 2000 television interview he was asked to select the person whom he thought to be 'the greatest writer of fiction of all time.' Crichton thought for a second and then replied, dryly and matter-of-factly, 'Sigmund Freud.'

The time has come to restore a wholesome view of the family as a basic institution, even if individual families may not live up to the standards that our social scientists expect of them. As social critic James Q. Wilson has recently written, our culture has seriously weakened the institution of the family in order to promote individualism at any cost.[9] In complex city societies, where various systems of belief and ethics exist, and are in constant competition with each other, people continue to perceive their membership in a family system as more directly meaningful to their lives than allegiance to the larger society. Although life in families is often emotionally difficult, the feeling nevertheless reverberates deep within us that the family system is still the most 'natural' one for us. When that system is lacking, or is faulty, individuals suffer as a result. In my view, the devaluation of the family may be the source of the *angst* and sense of alienation that many modern-day individuals feel, living as they do in large, impersonal social systems.

In his monumental 1909 study of social organization, the social theorist Charles H. Cooley defined kinship as the primary system of culture *par excellence*, giving stability and continuity to the activities of the tribe.[10] However defined, membership in a kinship unit provides every human being with a primary identity and a vital sense of belonging. That is why people tend to feel a 'kinship bond' when they meet a stranger of the same lineal descent, and why, at some point or other in their lives, many (if not most) people become interested in where the 'roots' of their 'family tree' lead. As the sociologist Max Weber (1864–1920) remarked, leadership in early tribal cultures tended to emerge typically from within kinship units because their communal activities revolved around the family with the most power and ability to withstand opposition from within the tribe.

The central feature of all kinship systems is the primary mother–child bond, to which diverse cultures have added different familial relations by the principle of descent, which connects one generation to the other in a systematic way and which determines certain rights and obligations across generations. Descent groups are traced typically through both sexes – that is, *bilaterally* – or through only the male or the female link – that is, *unilaterally*. In unilateral systems the descent is known as *patrilineal* if the derivation is through the male line, or *matrilineal* if it is through the female line. Anthropological surveys of kinship systems have shown in recent years that half of the world's cultures are patrilineal, one-third are bilateral, and the remainder are matrilineal. Bilateral kinship systems are characteristic of modern-day hunting-gathering tribes, such as the !Kung of the Kalahari Desert in southern Africa and the Inuit in northern Canada; and they are becoming increasingly characteristic of modern Western societies as well. Less frequent ways for tracing descent are the *parallel* system, in which males and females each trace their ancestry through their own sex, and the *cognatic* method, in which the relatives of both sexes are considered, with little formal distinction between them. Such systems are fundamental to the human way of life. None is better than any other. Each has its merits and demerits.

No matter what kinship system is in place in a society, the fact remains that it is the one to which we respond emotionally. I am convinced that the devaluation of the family as an institution has forced some troubled teens to look for alternatives to it. Joining a cult, for instance, reveals a hidden desire to be part of a highly organized system such as the family once was. Teens join cults so that they can immerse themselves in group life and thus leave decision making and all the pressures of growing up behind. It is easier to be told what to do than to have to act independently. We sometimes forget this, living in a culture that stresses independence and individuality. Humans are gregarious and emotionally interdependent beings. With notable exceptions – hermits and loners – individuals who cannot cope with the burdens of responsibility and individual decision making tend to join radical group formations. In effect, a cult acts like a surrogate family, offering the same kind of emotional shelter that the home is supposed to provide. That is why those who join cults become so totally committed to them – even to the point of ending up dead, as the most notorious cult-related incidents have made obvious in recent years.

Families in other parts of the world have not bought into the Freudian paradigm. Cultural traditions that support family cohesion, such as those in the Middle East, South Asia, and China, remain particularly strong, despite rapid change. A great majority of teenagers around the world experience close and functional relationships with their parents.[11]

The third line of attack is to expose media representations of adolescence and family life for what they are – convenient fictions. One convenient fiction – evident in movies such as *Animal House* (1978), *American Pie* (1999), and others like them – is that adolescence is all about rudeness, silliness, inanity, and sexual flirtation. Another fiction is that teens have street savvy and, especially, sex savvy. This theme pervades most of the pop-music lyrics of today. But nothing could be farther from the truth. Despite explicit sexuality in the media and specific instruction in sexuality by professional educators through straightforward discussions about sex in school, teens are apparently not processing what they hear and see. What they do know, they tend to pick up from peers.

Teens are largely immune to the sexuality that is all around them, given that it pertains to the adult world. Surveys taken in the year 2000 showed, in fact, that most of the almost 50 per cent of adolescents under the age of fifteen and 75 per cent of those under the age of nineteen who report having had sexual intercourse also report not having taken any precautions to protect themselves from disease or to avoid pregnancy. Pregnancy, AIDS, running away from home, and unparalleled physical dangers such as suicide, eating disorders, and the like, have now become common descriptors of adolescent life. The Centers for Disease Control and Prevention estimate that half of all new HIV infections in the United States are among people under the age of twenty-five. Statistics show that young people from all walks of life are having sex at younger and younger ages. Nearly one in ten reported having had sex before the age of thirteen in 2002, up 15 per cent from 1997 according to the Centers for Disease Control and Prevention Web site. And, according to the Henry J. Kaiser Family Foundation, despite a 20 per cent decrease in the teen birth rate between 1991 and 1999, 20 per cent of sexually active teen females get pregnant each year. Clearly, as the poet and critic Louise Bogan (1897–1970) has aptly put it, 'Childhood prolonged, cannot remain a fairyland; it becomes a hell.'[12]

Yet despite all the warnings and danger signs throughout the social order, people seem inclined to be duped by the media and the business world to hang on to their childish and youthful lifestyles. A recent example should suffice to make the point that juvenilization is a diffuse and ongoing phenomenon. In 2002, the Mattel Toy Company established a Planet Hot Wheels Web site where users can download a game. The site was aimed, clearly, at attracting young adults, whom children look up to. The Web site even offers upgrades for 'virtual vehicles' and a Motocross 1950s drag race – all free with a Hot Wheels purchase. In this way, the company is hoping to equate its childhood toy product with lifestyle cool, power, speed, and performance. As this example shows, grown-ups haven't outgrown their video games, which continue to be highly popular, especially with men in their twenties, thirties, and even forties. The names of the games have changed – from 1970s and 1980s names like Pac Man, Pitfall, and Pong to 2000 names like Gran Turismo, PlayStation, Grand Theft Auto, Final Fantasy X, Super Smash Bros. Melee, Metal Gear Solid, and Bond: Agent under Fire – but the market for them has not.

Recently, TV sitcoms and serials have shown a perverse fixation with the whole notion of family. In the series *The Sopranos*, family values are, strangely, symbolized by a weird, eccentric, and obnoxious clan. The appeal of the program lies, in my view, in the fact that the Sopranos are, none the less, a family – a fact that has not been missed by the hordes of academic pundits out there.[13] The same can be said about another bizarre TV program, *The Osbournes*. Ozzie Osbourne, a rock star who allegedly bit off the head of a bat in a concert and who led a lifestyle that included drug use and alcohol abuse, rendering him barely coherent, presides over a bunch of weirdos who nevertheless are bonded by family ties. All these TV representations show that we cherish the warmth and support that the family structure provides, even if that structure seems weird or bizarre.

System Failure

The time has come, clearly, to declare a cultural 'system failure.' To make our culture operational again, we must strive to create the conditions by which physical maturity will be expected to coincide with social maturity. This means spreading the message that growing up and growing old are okay! I started off my critique of our forever young culture by describing the 'groovy grandmother' I observed at the Grateful Dead concert in 1994 (chapter 1). Ironically, the only song of the Grateful Dead that made it to the top of the charts was 'Touch of Gray' (1987, *In the Dark*). The lyrics of that song are, significantly, about growing old and becoming wise.

According to a 1994 American census, the average life span of a human being living in North America is now approximately seventy-six years. Those in this age category constituted nearly 15 per cent of the population in the year 2002. That figure is expected to rise to 20 per cent by 2030. Old people are going to be everywhere one turns. For this reason, the Grateful Dead's advice will have to be taken seriously. Above all else, we will have to dispel the many myths about old age that have crystallized in our forever young culture.[14] They include the view of aging as a period of decline and thus of the need for older people to withdraw from society. Another is the view that older adults become silly and unbalanced – a view spread by silly movies about 'grumpy old men,' such as those starring the late Walter Matthau, and by the widespread use of disparaging words in reference to old age (*old fart, old geezer*, etc.). The fact that derogatory expressions referring to old people abound in our language indicates how ubiquitous ageism has become. This is nothing but a symptom of the FYS. History is replete with examples of older adults being as creative as when they were young, if not more so. Giuseppe Verdi (1813–1901) composed his two greatest masterpieces, *Otello* and *Falstaff*, in his eighties; writer May Sarton (1912–95) and painter Marcel Duchamp (1887–1968) did likewise in their own artistic domains. While it is true that certain attributes (memory, speed, visual-motor flexibility) decline with age, this decline is compensated by what was once called the 'wisdom of age.'

How did our negativism about age come about? As discussed in the opening chapter, the source of many of our modern-day myths with regard to age and aging is the juvenilization process that took hold of cultural groupthink in the latter part of the nineteenth century, when a gradually increasing economic affluence set this process in motion. For the first time in history, a single economic system – the one that took shape after the Industrial Revolution – was capable of guaranteeing a certain level of affluence to increasingly larger segments of society. With more wealth and leisure time at their disposal, common people were more able to live the good life. And with the economic capacity to improve the chances of staying healthier, and thus of living much longer than previous generations, a desire to preserve youth for a much longer period of life started to define the collective state of mind. This desire was nurtured by the messages that bombarded society from radio and print advertising in the early part of the twentieth century – messages that became more persuasive and widespread with the advent of television in the early 1950s. By the 1960s, the desire to be 'young' meant the desire not only to stay and look healthier for longer but also to act and think differently from 'older' people. In 2002, Pepsi mounted a truly revealing campaign in this regard, showing the company's ability to tap into cultural groupthink. Ads and commercials blurted out that Pepsi was the drink that remains 'forever young.' This message is something that reverberates with meaning because our culture no longer sees the difference between young and old and, indeed, as argued throughout this book, attempts to distort it. In 2000, the U.S. Census found that nearly 4 million people between twenty-five and thirty-four live with their parents, that the average age for a first marriage is twenty-six (in 1970 it was twenty-two), and that childbearing is postponed to the mid-thirties. Pepsi's forever young message is simply a mirror of what is going on – and a fractured one at that.

Even though families nowadays stay together longer, the root cause of the disrespect shown towards the elderly is, paradoxically, the modern family itself or, more accurately, the devalued institution that still goes under the name *family*. A society that devalues the family will, simply put, also devalue its elders. But the times 'are a-changing' (again), as Bob Dylan so aptly put it in the counter-culture era. Contrary to what is suggested in television shows ranging from *Frasier* to *The West Wing*, commitment among married people is not fleeting, and happy marriages are not rare – nor should they be. The effect of family breakups on teenagers is inestimable. Virtually all the teens of divorced parents I have interviewed over the years have found the breakup of their family to be agonizing. Some portray it as 'caused by them,' others as something 'done to them.' Very few see it neutrally as a private matter between two adults. In such cases, teens are at risk in more ways than our family experts can imagine.

Particularly worrisome are the dangers that teens running away from home face. Parents have frequently told me that they felt like prisoners in their own house – slaves to the whims of their teens – but that they preferred this to having their sons or daughters leave home to face the danger of the streets. And their fears are not unfounded: a million teens run away from home every year; the teen homicide rate has increased by 232 per cent since 1950; one million teenage girls become pregnant yearly, most of them living away from home. Something is terribly wrong here. There is, of course, no single reason why teens run away. Family conflicts, peer lifestyles that are conducive to 'living on the streets,' a need to cut the 'umbilical cord' decisively, and so on, are all factors. It all depends on the individual and on the situation. But it is my sense that a good family life, based on shared responsibilities and trust, will at least provide a basis for the runaway to re-enter the home.

In addition to an increase in disrespect for the elderly and in the number of divorces, another sure sign of system failure is the unprecedented emergence of eating disorders among adolescents. Anorexia nervosa – a disorder characterized by an abnormal fear of becoming obese – is caused by a distorted sense of body image induced by media representations. As incredible to the Western mind as it may appear, researchers have found that there simply is no such thing as anorexia nervosa among some peoples, such as Malaysians and Native Americans. The disease clearly has a cultural origin. No standard therapy for it exists – nor can one exist, given its cultural etiology.[15]

Another truly tragic sign of system failure is the increase in suicide among teens. Suicide is the second leading cause of death, after accidents, among white adolescents aged fifteen to twenty-four, according to statistics published by the U.S. Department of Health in 2001. The suicide rate has tripled since the 1950s. The causes of suicide have, of course, been studied by social and behavioural scientists. From their research, it is obvious to me that teen suicide is virtually unpredictable, although four factors in particular seem to place an adolescent at risk: (1) suffering from low self-esteem or an emotional problem; (2) being under stress as a result of school-related, romantic, or peer-related problems; (3) experiencing family disruption or family conflict; and (4) having had a friend who committed suicide.

What really brings about the decision to terminate one's life? Certainly, one can see depression, loss of social status, and inability to cope with uncertainty, among others, as 'causes.' But many people face similar situations and dilemmas without ending up suicidal. There may be genetic factors involved. It is certainly not for me to give any expert opinion on this truly devastating problem. Let me simply say that the question of suicide comes up frequently in teen interviews. I have found that truly troubled young people will attempt to tell someone that they are contemplating a drastic solution to their problems. Most adolescents think seriously about the *meaning* of life. But our society, as a whole, seems to have little time for, or interest in, discussing 'life's greater questions' with adolescents – or with anyone, for that matter. This creates feelings of 'emptiness' and 'disconnection' from reality that are widespread among adolescents. Many simply attempt to cope with their life as best they can; in a few extreme cases, suicide presents itself as an escape route. The fixation on suicide as a kind of definitive answer to the feeling of disconnection is, in fact, a recurrent theme in some of the music lyrics that adolescents have often listened to. The songs of such bands as Nine Inch Nails and Nirvana, to mention but two, are about despair, bleakness, dissatisfaction, and alienation. Expressions such as 'I'd rather die,' 'my hatred grows extreme,' 'my head is filled with disease,' 'I really don't know who I am,' and 'this world of piss' are found in the lyrics of Nine Inch Nails. They express the *angst* that some adolescents feel, alienated from a culture that places more value on the consumption of goods than on the questions that confront them from within. In 1994, Nirvana's lead singer, Kurt Cobain, committed suicide, showing a whole generation that his words were not vacuous, that he meant what he said.

As a historical aside, it is worth noting that the whole notion of *alienation* was developed originally by Karl Marx (1818–83) to explain the estrangement of human beings from their society,[16] although it was a term previously used by Georg Wilhelm Friedrich Hegel (1770–1831) and other Romantic philosophers who saw the estrangement as a matter of individual *angst*. Closely associated with this concept is Émile Durkheim's notion of anomie,[17] which he saw as being caused by rapid economic growth and prosperity.

Another root cause of suicide among adolescents is undoubtedly extreme sensitivity to peer relations and conflicts. Ostracism from peer groups or constant ridiculing by peers is what brought about the homicide–suicide pact that took place at Columbine High School in Colorado in 1999. The two students in that case murdered a number of their peers and then took their own lives. 'Getting even' for the constant ridicule they suffered appears to have been their primary motivation.

In his controversial 1999 book, *The Rise and Fall of the American Teenager*, Thomas Hine, with no tongue in cheek, attributes the increase in suicide and violence to the unnecessarily long period of education that keeps young people in a dangerous 'holding pattern.'[18] In effect, Hine puts the blame on obligatory high school education as a major source of our current system failure. But the high schools, in and of themselves, can hardly be held responsible. They are mirrors of the culture that they serve. Paradoxically, compulsory education came about not only to impart knowledge and skill, but also to solve problems of crime and drug use. In the latter part of the nineteenth century, social reformers believed (naïvely, in hindsight) that education was the solution to all ills, because it would take dispossessed and poor youths off the streets, thus preserving social stability and preventing crime, alcohol abuse, and poverty. By 1918, all U.S. states had passed compulsory school attendance laws. How ironic it is that today many American social critics, like Hine, blame the institution that was established to eliminate the very problems they decry! The reformers believed that a school system for all would create common bonds among an increasingly diverse population. They argued that free elementary school education should be made available to everyone, through public funds, and that schools should be accountable both to local school boards and to state governments. They also argued for the establishment of compulsory school attendance laws for children of elementary school age. By the end of the nineteenth century, the reformers had largely achieved their objectives.

In 1900, high school was still the privilege of the rich. Only 10 per cent of American adolescents aged fourteen to seventeen were enrolled in high schools. Most of them were from affluent families. After the introduction of strict child-labour laws in the early twentieth century, fewer adolescents entered the workforce than previously. This gave them an opportunity to attend school. School provided adolescents with an acceptable alternative to labour before they entered the workforce, established a family, or began college. As the twentieth century progressed, most states enacted legislation making education compulsory to age sixteen. The rise in the graduation rate from American high schools was one of the most striking developments in education during the twentieth century. From 1900 to 1996, the percentage of adolescents who graduated from high school increased from about 6 per cent to over 85 per cent.

The movement to make high school education compulsory was based on a naïve view that schooling could successfully address a host of social concerns. High schools were seen not only as places where students could prepare for the practical demands of everyday life but also as places for youth to experience the coming-of-age period with peers. High schools thus came to assume the double function of educating students to fit into North American society while providing opportunities for them to break out from whatever social or economic circumstances constrained their development.

But, as the Scottish poet Robert Burns (1759–96) so aptly put it, it would seem that 'the best laid schemes o' Mice an' Men,' rarely work out, leaving 'nought but grief an' pain, / For promis'd joy!'[19] During the 1980s and 1990s, virtually all U.S. states gave unprecedented legislative attention to raising high school education standards, as a result of the publication of a federal report in 1983 that detected alarmingly low academic achievement in high schools. This report, titled *A Nation at Risk*, presented statistics suggesting that American students were outperformed on international academic tests by students from other industrial societies. The study also reported that U.S. test scores were declining across the board. Many parents, educators, and government officials believed that only a concerted, centralized reform effort could overcome the apparent shortcomings of U.S. education. Because the perceived 'crisis in education' was based largely on test-score results, most states subsequently implemented reform strategies that emphasized more frequent testing and more state-mandated curriculum requirements. Similar steps were taken in Canada, especially in Alberta and Ontario. This 'return-to-basics' movement culminated in 2002 with President George W. Bush's enactment of legislation designed to bring the school system back into the 'regulatory' frame of mind that had motivated its initial *raison d'être*.

What the 'back-to-basics' movement has overlooked, however, are the unfounded assumptions that inspired compulsory schooling in the first place. From its inception, the high school was seen not just as a place of learning but, more importantly, as a place to keep adolescents at bay – in a 'holding pattern,' as Hine so aptly puts it. The negative consequences of this assumption have become obvious. It constitutes, perhaps, the greatest factor contributing to the current failure of our system. It is ironic to note that an institution that was set up to solve social problems is now itself beset by many of those same social problems. To be sure, the high schools are filled with adolescents studying hard. But it is also true to say that they face a challenge to be that way. Violence at school, shootings, and increased aggression in the school-yard have made people reconsider the role of education in the adolescent's life. Instead of seeking a 'return-to-basics' solution, or some other media-popularized or politically motivated solution, I believe that, as never before, schools need to think of themselves as something other than primarily solvers of social problems. Unless there is a radical shift in society, the school can no longer be everything to everyone. This does not mean that schools will have to redesign their curricula radically, or rethink their basic pedagogical practices; rather, it means that they will have to reinterpret the role that they should play in our society.

In field work I conducted in 1998–2000, I found that the teens who are most adjusted to the academic life of the school and who go to school to develop their skills, not just to be with peers, are those in 'special' or 'alternative' schools. For example, I visited several 'schools for the arts' in major North American cities. Such schools offer students the opportunity to engage in artistic programs that suit their personalities, natural talents, and career aspirations. In other words, they allow students to learn what they themselves feel is best, not just what adults want them to learn. Virtually all the students of such schools whom I spoke to told me that they enjoy going to school because they are doing what they do and love best. Not only that, their 'joy of learning' seems to spill over into the other, more traditional courses that they are generally required to take (English, math, history, etc.). As a consequence, they tend to do better than they otherwise might, and they realize concretely that such knowledge has a role to play in their lives as adults. Socialization in such schools is seen as intertwined with the goals of the curriculum. Students socialize without cliquing; their friends are perceived to be partners in the overall academic goals of the school. Follow-up interviews with teachers and parents indicated to me that they, too, are highly satisfied with the type of schooling involved. Some parents worried about their teens' entry into college or into society because of the perceived 'low career value' of the arts; but, by and large, they also understood that their teens are progressing much better than they would otherwise.

This pattern of findings stands in stark contrast to those from similar interviews I conducted with students in 'regular' schools. These are schools where classes consist of groups of twenty to thirty students with a teacher at the front of the room; instruction proceeds by lecture, demonstration, discussion, or silent work at a desk; and teachers often assign homework for the students to complete after class. Most of the students in these schools see the school environment as a threat to their 'physical survival,' not as a place to hone their intellect. No wonder teens form cliques in such places. Cliques offer shelter and safety. That is why those left out of cliques can become so devastated and fearful that they end up sometimes taking drastic action, as witnessed by school shootings and killings such as those at Columbine High School in Colorado in 1999. Such drastic and tragic reactions are, in effect, perpetrated by despondent teens wanting to 'get even.'

My follow-up interviews with teachers suggest that they are aware of everything that is going on, by and large. But they feel powerless, because they sense that the cultural forces at work in the school are beyond their control. In my view, the teachers in such schools today are valiant gladiators fighting a losing battle. My interviews with the parents of the teenagers in such schools suggest that they expect more of the school than the school is able to provide.

The high school clearly needs to be endowed with a new sense of purpose, and perhaps given a broad mandate to pursue many of the goals of the so-called alternative schools. Efficiency at solving quadratic equations is not perceived as cool or personality-enhancing by many teens. But the means to make such a skill appealing are probably right before our very eyes. If alternative schools are indeed more successful in producing well-adjusted adolescent learners, then it is probably because they make academic achievement an attractive end in itself within the school environment, by allowing the students to develop their individual talents.

Needless to say, there are a host of problems associated with such schools that are beyond the present discussion. But if there is one lesson well worth learning, it is simply that these schools have been successful in removing the 'fear' factor by allowing students to pursue what they are most inclined to do. Perhaps schools specializing in math and science, others in the humanities, and so on, should be instituted. After all, that has been the extant model in many parts of Europe, where violence at school tends to be far less of a problem than it is in North America.

The idea of teaching specific subjects to all children and adolescents may have run its course and outlived its usefulness. In ancient cultures, the goal of teachers – usually priests, shamans, or elders – was to determine which kinds of functional skills and knowledge should be taught to the children and youth of a society, in tandem with its needs and beliefs. Learners incapable of developing certain types of knowledge and skills were assigned social roles that were deemed more consistent with their abilities. There was no concept of teaching all things to all children, although the oldest known systems of education did teach religion and the traditions of the people to all the younger members of a society. At the beginning of the twentieth century, education was greatly influenced by the writings of the Swedish educator Ellen Key, whose book *The Century of the Child* (1900) inspired progressive educators in various countries to transform the existing educational practices into a system of teaching based on the needs and potentials of the child rather than on the needs of society or the precepts of religion. Especially influential in the United States in adopting this paradigm was the philosopher and educator John Dewey (1859–1952), who stressed the holistic development of the child in terms of the individual's needs and interests.

In contrast to a focus on the learner's needs, however, Western education has, by and large, taken its main thrust in the twentieth century from what is often called 'Descartes's project.' In 1637, the philosopher René Descartes (1596–1650) elaborated the view that education should centre its activities on teaching children how to think logically, by showing them how to classify knowledge into neat little boxes – from which we have derived the modern idea of teaching separate subjects at specific times of the day, on a regular basis, to all learners. But if the current crisis in education has taught us anything worthwhile, it is that such grand schemes overlook the fact that students bring to the classroom different personalities, needs, expectations, and talents. The student is not a 'monolith'; each one arrives in class with a perception of self interwoven into his or her natural abilities. The interviews I conducted, along with a spate of recent motivational studies, show that adolescents find a learning syllabus tailored to adult priorities of little or no interest. On the other hand, they perceive ideas and processes that relate to their own peculiar types of abilities and talents as much more meaningful.

Having said all this, I am quite aware that, short of making schooling optional during the adolescent years, there are no simple solutions, no magical formulas, no recipes for solving our current system failure. Perhaps the educational bureaucracy has become so Byzantine and self-serving that it is beyond repair and transformation. I certainly hope not. Moreover, I have found that institutions have a knack of working out solutions by themselves.

During my research projects, I noticed that teenagers universally responded to poetry and to other creative products of the imagination (music, drama, etc.), when these were put in relation to their emotional and social experiences. I also found that schools that focused more on the traditional 'humanistic' subjects tended to stimulate in their learners a love of all learning. This is actually the approach to learning that the ancient Greeks cherished. They did not see any need to separate the study of mathematics from the study of philosophy or poetry. On the contrary, they believed that a true love of learning would emerge when a balance was achieved among the arts, philosophy, and the sciences. They also firmly believed that education was necessarily tied to larger social and personal realities. In sum, the current crisis in education has made it obvious that the school can no longer act alone, apart from the family, the working world, and other institutions, in solving society's problems.

Restoring Continuity

At the start of the twentieth century, the sociologist Émile Durkheim (1858–1917) suggested, as mentioned above, that anomie (alienation) was the main cause of suicide. He traced the roots of this modern-day psychic disease to affluence, implying that the Western world's blatant materialism had created the social conditions that ineluctably induced an all-pervading sense of rootlessness and 'discontinuity' within our spiritual selves. This discontinuity, Durkheim claimed, led to feelings of anxiety and dissatisfaction.[20] In turn, those feelings led some individuals, Durkheim warned, to find a way out of their psychic *angst* by taking their own lives. In my view, Durkheim's notion of alienation might explain not only the increase in suicide among teens but also the constant penchant for rebellion among modern-day youth in general. In a sense, the adolescent years are all about alienation. This is a theme that has been captured by the TV sitcom (of all things) *Buffy the Vampire Slayer*. The teens on that program wrestle with alienation, isolation, and, above all, spirituality. The plots revolve around fantasy themes, but the show always digs deeper to reveal the underpinnings beneath our myths and fairy tales. No wonder it has had such a broad appeal among the young, even if it perpetuates, in my opinion, the *Sturm und Drang* view in a contemporary (albeit enlightened) guise.[21] The program is also attractive to viewers because it exploits pop culture's love of several genres at once – superheroes, a comic-book style of delivery, and disenfranchisement (an age group nobody takes seriously). The sitcom revolves around the theme of horror. But it is not the horror depicted in traditional narrative. Rather, it is the horror that the high school scene has become – a world of nasty cliques, of anti-intellectualism, of coolness, and of inane adult bureaucratic structures. Buffy's father has deserted the family, and her mother is largely 'clueless' about what is going on in young people's lives. In 2001, Buffy went on to college, where, seemingly, more maturity and sanity exist.

Fans of the show have proved extraordinarily dedicated to it: they support a Buffy industry that already produces the obligatory T-shirts, posters, trading cards, and jewellery, a quarterly magazine, books about the show, and scores of magazine articles and Web sites. Its appeal lies, in my view, in the fact that the program portrays average kids, in average relationships, battling the forces of adolescent evil, personified by vampires, demons, and monsters.

One of the show's central subtexts, as I read it, is that teens need their parents and their teachers much more than they need peers. Alienation can occur within the home; but it is more likely to occur outside it. Significantly, a 1998 *New York Times* and CBS News survey found that although 55 per cent of teens agree that there are times they feel it is necessary to talk to their parents about critical things in their lives, four out of five did not do so because they were sure that their parents 'wouldn't understand,' or else were too busy with their own lives to care. No wonder that teens develop their own enclaves, with their own sets of values and ethics.[22]

In this book, I have made a distinction among physical, social, and personal forms of maturity. The subtext I have tried to interlace throughout is that there is an imbalance among the three brought about by the invention of adolescence as a social experiment in the nineteenth century – an experiment given 'scientific legitimacy' by psychology and sustained by the media-entertainment oligarchy throughout the twentieth century. The roots of alienation, I would claim, are to be found in that imbalance. The time to restore a balance between the physical, social, and personal forms of maturation by declaring the experiment a failure is, clearly, long overdue.

As an aside, I find rather alarming the new 'trend' of attempting to explain adolescent problems in biological terms. It is a misguided trend, epitomized recently by the work of Steven Pinker.[23] It is now being used to support the notion that depression is connected to brain growth at adolescence. In 2002, the National Institutes of Mental Health (NIMH) estimated that 8 per cent of adolescents and 2 per cent of children (some as young as four) have symptoms of depression.[24] As usual, American medicine is looking for the 'source' of such 'diseases of the spirit' in human biology. Journals and TV programs now blurt out that it's all in the brain.

The evidence against this new 'biological' attempt to explain away adolescence is overwhelming. Luigi Luca Cavalli-Sforza and Francesco Cavalli-Sforza, for instance, have shown that no such depressions occur among the youth of contemporary Pygmy society.[25] Life expectancy at birth, in that society, is an incredible seventeen years. The 'young' in that society hardly have the time to go through an adolescent form of depression due to brain physiology.

Obviously, change must come. The prolonged period of adolescence leading to the symptomatology that I have called the FYS in our society must simply be eliminated. But, one may legitimately ask, from where will the impetus for change come? In my view, it has already started among the young people themselves. From my interviews and daily interactions with them, I sense a 'mature' mood in their behaviour and conversations. They are starting to get involved more and more in the arts, finding out that a symphony from the pen of an adolescent Mozart has much more to say to them than do the panderings and 'put-ons' of an Eminem, a Britney Spears, a Ja Rule, or whoever else may be catapulted to centre stage by the adult managers of cool. Although a large segment of the adolescent population continues to live in a virtual fog, many teens tell me that they are tired of being manipulated by the media-entertainment industry. One teen put it to me bluntly as follows: 'Do the media guys really think they can fool us with the grossness and derangement of *South Park* and *Disposable Teens* [a video by Marilyn Manson]?' Another aptly critiqued the self-serving egoism of the sitcom *Ally McBeal*: 'That show is supposed to help us understand people today. It's sick. Who really wants to be like Ally?' As of early 2002, that show was losing its young viewers – viewers who became mature enough to see through the self-moralizing inanity of the program. After five years, the love affair with Ally McBeal came to an end, as Fox cancelled the series in 2002. People had had enough of the neuroses of 'forever young' adults.

Statistics bear out that the world is 'a-changing,' to quote Bob Dylan again. As Neil Howe and William Strauss reported in 2000, information gathered in the late 1990s bears this out.[26] To wit: the number of killings and suicides in all American schools at all grade levels during the period 1992–2000 shows that there were fifty-five in 1992 and only twelve in 2000; the U.S. divorce rate peaked in 1980 at 23 per cent, diminishing to 19 per cent in 1996. Significantly, the rates of drug-overdose fatalities by age were 0.8 per cent for ages fifteen to nineteen and 1 per cent for ages forty to forty-four in 1979; in 1996, the rate remained virtually unchanged for ages fifteen to nineteen at 1.2 per cent but went up dramatically to 12.6 per cent for ages forty to forty-four. Who is more mature here?

Some say that the impetus for change started on 11 September 2001, when the World Trade Center towers were brought to the ground by terrorists and nearly 3,000 people died for no sane reason. That event, it is claimed, brought about a quick sobering of mood throughout Western culture and started a process of maturation. Perhaps. But in order for society to 'grow up,' it will have to restore importance to basic institutions, such as the family, and not rely constantly on the advice of experts in psychology and sociology on matters of upbringing.[27] Humans can change anything they want, even the very systems of everyday life in which they are reared. Such systems can be compared to the default mode of computer software. This format can be changed intentionally by a human programmer, if he or she so desires. Analogously, our media-generated and media-sustained forever young format can be changed, if the will is there to do so.

This is, in fact, what some enlightened individuals and groups are now attempting to do. The Canadian activist Kalle Lasn, for instance, has started a truly radical campaign against the globalization of consumerist culture.[28] As a leading voice in the so-called culture-jamming movement, Lasn (who is the founder of *Adbusters* magazine, which satirizes ads and commercials) is in the vanguard of a new mood that decries the mindless consumerism of modern society. Culture jammers are a loose global network of media activists aiming to change the way media and corporate institutions wield power. Lasn believes that corporate America is no longer a country but one overarching 'brand' shaped by the cult of celebrity and the spectacles that sustain it. Culture and marketing are, according to Lasn, one and the same.

Lasn's fears are not unfounded. Today, the global distraction factory is operated by a tiny number of colossal media conglomerates, such as the Disney Corporation, AOL Time Warner, and Sony. Global advertising is now under the control of, basically, a handful of advertising agencies based in New York, London, Paris, and Tokyo. Lasn is joined by other leading young intellectuals who argue that market populism has been good for business but bad for the communal soul. I mention Thomas Frank and Naomi Klein as two such intellectuals.[29] Aware of the social dangers that such a state of affairs poses, Lasn has issued a 'Media Manifesto,' in obvious parallel with many other subversive manifestos that have been issued in the past (of which Karl Marx's is probably the most famous).

However, well-meaning though such groups and individuals are, we cannot bring about change simply by blaming global capitalism for all our problems. We must not forget that it was the capitalist system that brought democracy to Europe in the first place by allowing common folk the opportunity to become wealthy and, thus, to stand up to the hegemony of the religious order of medieval times.[30] Although it has become itself a bizarre religion, strangely blending puritanical religious values with pop-culture mores, capitalism has never taken the drastic measures that the religious order did in attempting to preserve its control of society. After all, it is up to the individual in a capitalist democracy to simply say 'No.' There is nothing more effective, in my view, than personal choice.

Incidentally, it is somewhat ironic to note that those who most condemn the media are the ones most inclined to use it for their own purposes. Take, for example, the vociferous 'religious right' groups in the United States who are wont to blame the media for all that ails the country. Yet the leaders of that movement use television to great advantage themselves. Through the despised 'tube,' they purvey their ideas and their own products (videos, CDs, etc.), promising salvation and comfort to their viewers. Televangelism is a perfect example of how the very people who condemn the media use it for their own ends. The scary part is that many of these characters have the full support of some business moguls. Indeed, in 1988, one such televangelist, Pat Robertson, ran for president of the United States with the support of various media moguls, including Rupert Murdoch. Robertson's religious fanaticism was well known, since he claimed to speak in tongues and have direct access to God. The media culture in which we live is a strange one indeed!

The media are, as mentioned throughout this book, sources of distraction and engagement at the same time, blurring the line between the two. But this is not unique to the modern world. The operas of Giuseppe Verdi, great as they are, had an initial distraction function – people went to them to be entertained, plain and simple. The fact that his music rose above its entertainment function is a consequence of various factors, not the least of which is the musical genius of the com poser. Everyone in our mediated world can easily locate a jingle such as the Alka Seltzer one ('Plop, plop, fizz, fizz, oh what a relief it is') at the distraction end, and a CD recording of a musical work such as Mozart's powerful *Requiem Mass* at the other. This line of reasoning brings out concretely that people, by and large, can discern quality in the smorgasbord of options that our media culture makes available.

There are no simple answers, no easy solutions. Cultures resolve their problems and set their future goals dynamically and synergistically *from within*. While it is true that the global village has transformed the world into a consumer-frenzied distraction factory with megacompanies controlling its operation, it is also true that constant changes to this factory are coming from within, making it unstable at best. Economics alone cannot run a society forever.

The Picture of Dorian Gray

The dangers posed by the desire to hold on to 'beautiful youth' were brought out dramatically in the nineteenth century by the great Irish writer Oscar Wilde (1854–1900) in his only novel, *The Picture of Dorian Gray* (1891). The character Dorian Gray had a portrait painted of himself. He saw in his own countenance the face of Adonis. The handsome aesthete thus exclaimed, 'Why should it keep what I must lose? Every moment that passes takes something from me, and gives something to it? Oh, if it were only the other way! If the picture could change, and I could be always what I am now!'[31] Dorian Gray's perverse aspiration was strangely fulfilled. He abandoned himself to every pleasure that his profligate mind could devise, yet he never aged. It was upon the portrait locked away in his attic that the marks of degeneration mysteriously appeared. Our contemporary world has, in a metaphorical sense, become one huge 'picture of Dorian Gray,' as it continues 'on the outside' to perpetrate adolescent aesthetics and lifestyles as the aesthetics and lifestyles of all.

The time has come to take a close look at that picture. Like Dorian, we too have hidden our degeneration in the attic. We have been mesmerized by youth for too long, and our fascination with it is becoming both wearisome and worrisome. It is simply unwise to continue in this way. There are alternatives. As the Israeli politician Abba Eban (1915–) aptly put it in 1970, history 'teaches us that men and nations behave wisely once they have exhausted all other alternatives.'[32] The final word of wisdom, however, belongs to the Grateful Dead, whose 1994 concert led me to write this book in the first place. As they put it in their 1987 hit 'Touch of Gray,' 'It's OK to grow old.'

Notes

Chapter 1. The Fountain of Youth

1 Marcel Danesi, *Giambattista Vico and the Cognitive Science Enterprise* (New York: Peter Lang, 1995).

2 See, for instance, L.S. Vygotsky, *Thought and Language* (Cambridge, MA: MIT Press, 1961).

3 Helen E. Fisher, *Anatomy of Love* (New York: Norton, 1992), 233.

4 S. Shahar, *Childhood in the Middle Ages* (London: Routledge, 1992), 27.

5 Stanley G. Hall, *Adolescence* (New York: Appleton-Century-Crofts, 1904).

6 E.H. Erikson, *Childhood and Society* (New York: Norton, 1950); *Identity: Youth and Crisis* (New York: Norton, 1968).

7 The term became popular as a result of the play *Sturm und Drang* by Friedrich Maximilian von Klinger (1752–1831), becoming the catchphrase to designate a German romantic literary movement whose works typically depicted the struggles of a highly emotional individual against conventional society.

8 Margaret Mead, *Coming of Age in Samoa* (New York: North American Library, 1928); and *From the South Seas: Studies of Adolescence and Sex in Primitive Societies* (New York: Morrow, 1939).

9 Few topics attract more attention from scholars and researchers today, from within and outside psychology, than the topic of adolescence and youth culture. Of the works that I have consulted in order to gain insights during the writing of this book, I mention the following: J.E. Coté and A.L. Allahar, *Generation on Hold: Coming of Age in the Late Twentieth Century* (Toronto: Stoddart, 1994); H.J. Graff, *Conflicting Paths: Growing Up in America* (Cambridge, MA: Harvard University Press, 1995); Grace Palladino, *Teenagers: An American History* (New York: Basic Books, 1996); Patricia Hersch, *A Tribe*

Apart: A Journey into the Heart of American Adolescence (New York: Fawcett, 1998); Thomas Hine, *The Rise and Fall of the American Teenager* (New York: Bard Books, 1999); W. Mueller, *Understanding Today's Youth Culture* (New York: Tyndale, 1999); and D. Pountain and D. Robins, *Cool Rules: Anatomy of an Attitude* (New York: Reaktion Books, 2000).

10 Recent historical analyses of adolescence that bring out implicit cultural biases in this domain are Palladino, *Teenagers*; Hersch, *A Tribe Apart*; and Hine, *Rise and Fall of the American Teenager*.

11 Gail Sheehy, *New Passages: Mapping Your Life across Time* (New York: Ballantine, 1995).

12 Stuart Ewen, *All Consuming Images* (New York: Basic Books, 1988), 20.

13 R.S. Lynd and H.M. Lynd, *Middletown: A Study in Modern American Culture* (New York: Harcourt, Brace, and World, 1929), 29.

14 Roland Barthes, *Mythologies* (Paris: Seuil, 1957).

15 Plato, *The Republic*, ed. C.M. Blackwell (New York: Charles Scribner's Sons, 1956), 234.

16 T. Greenwald, *Rock and Roll* (New York: Friedman, 1992), 85.

17 On this point, see J. Queenan, *Balsamic Dreams: A Short but Self-Important History of the Baby Boomer Generation* (New York: Henry Holt, 2000).

18 Douglas Owram, *Born at the Right Time: A History of the Baby Boom Generation* (Toronto: University of Toronto Press, 1996).

19 Bruce Pollock, *Hipper Than Our Kids: A Rock and Roll Journal of the Baby Boom Generation* (New York: Schirmer, 1993), 2.

20 W. Irwin, M.T. Conrad, and A.J. Skoble (eds), *'The Simpsons' and Philosophy* (Chicago: Open Court, 2001).

21 A. Goodwin, *Dancing in the Distraction Factory: Music Television and Popular Culture* (Minneapolis: University of Minnesota Press, 1992).

22 Frank Thomas, *The Conquest of Cool* (Chicago: University of Chicago Press, 1997).

23 See, on this point, J. Lopiano-Misdom and J. De Luca, *Street Trends: How Today's Alternative Youth Cultures Are Creating Tomorrow's Mainstream Markets* (New York: Harper Business, 1997).

24 David Crystal, *Language and the Internet* (Cambridge: Cambridge University Press, 2001).

25 See also Guy Merchant, 'Teenagers in Cyberspace: An Investigation of Language Use and Language Change in Internet Chatrooms,' *Journal of Research in Reading* 24 (2001): 293–306.

26 See, for example, K.V. Hachinski and V. Hachinski, 'Music and the Brain,' *Canadian Medical Association Journal* 151 (1994): 293–5; and C. Holden, 'Random Samples: Smart Music,' *Science* 266 (1995): 968–9.

Chapter 2. Looking like Teenagers

1 Helen E. Fisher, *Anatomy of Love* (New York: Norton, 1992), 272–3.
2 See, on this point, an interesting book by Grant McCracken, *Big Hair: A Journey into the Transformation of Self* (Toronto: Penguin, 1995).
3 See Sherrie Inness, *Tough Girls: Women Warriors and Wonder Women in Popular Culture* (Philadelphia: University of Pennsylvania Press, 1998).
4 See, on this topic, Simona Chiose, *Good Girls Do: Sex Chronicles of a Shameless Generation* (Toronto: ECW Press, 2001), and Catharine Driscoll, *Girls: Feminine Adolescence in Popular Culture and Cultural Theory* (New York: Columbia University Press, 2002).
5 The high number of works on gang and cult membership published yearly is evidence that such membership has become a worrisome problem. See, for example, M. Webb, *Coping with Street Gangs* (New York: Rosen Publishing Group, 1990); K.M. Porterfield, *Straight Talk about Cults* (New York: Facts on File, 1997); and R.W. Bibby and D.C. Posterski, *Teen Trends* (Toronto: Stoddart, 2000).
6 See the excellent treatment of this topic by Marjorie Heins, *Not in Front of the Children: Indecency, Censorship and the Innocence of Youth* (New York: Hill and Wang, 2001).
7 The enormous number of books published in the last few decades on body image and its consequences is an 'alarm signal.' See, for example, H. Bruch, *The Golden Cage: The Enigma of Anorexia Nervosa* (Cambridge, MA: Harvard University Press, 1978); J.J. Brumberg, *Fasting Girls: The Emergence of Anorexia Nervosa as a Modern Disease* (Cambridge, MA: Harvard University Press, 1988); M. Pipher, *Reviving Ophelia: Saving the Selves of Adolescent Girls* (New York: Ballantine, 1995); M. Hornbacher, *Wasted: A Memoir of Anorexia and Bulimia* (New York: Harper Flamingo, 1998); and S. Azam, *Rebel, Rogue, Mischievous Babe: Stories about Being a Powerful Girl* (Toronto: HarperCollins, 2001).
8 Jordan Goodman, *Tobacco in History: The Cultures of Dependence* (London: Routledge, 1993).
9 Richard Klein, *Cigarettes Are Sublime* (Durham: Duke University Press, 1993).
10 Michael E. Starr, 'The Marlboro Man: Cigarette Smoking and Masculinity in America,' *Journal of Popular Culture* 12 (1984): 45–56.
11 Reported by *The Wall Street Journal*, 4 October 2002.
12 Michel Foucault, *The History of Sexuality*, vol. 1 (London: Allen Lane, 1976).
13 Kathy Peiss, *Hope in a Jar: The Making of America's Beauty Culture* (New York: Metropolitan Books, 1998).

14 Vance Packard, *The Hidden Persuaders* (New York: McKay, 1957).

15 J.B. Twitchell, *Twenty Ads That Shook the World* (New York: Crown, 2000), 1.

16 Marshall McLuhan, *Understanding Media* (London: Routledge and Kegan Paul, 1964).

17 This was discussed not only by Packard but also by Bryan Wilson Key in a series of attention-grabbing books in the 1970s and 1980s: *Subliminal Seduction* (New York: Signet, 1972), *Media Sexploitation* (New York: Signet, 1976), *The Clam-Plate Orgy* (New York: Signet, 1980), and *The Age of Manipulation* (New York: Holt, 1989).

18 Naomi Klein, *No Logo: Taking Aim at the Brand Bullies* (Toronto: Alfred A. Knopf, 2000).

19 Virginia Woolf, *Orlando* (New York: Modern Library, 1929), 124.

Chapter 3. Talking like Teenagers

1 Edward Sapir, *Language* (New York: Harcourt Brace, 1921).

2 Benjamin Lee Whorf, *Language in Thought and Reality*, ed. J.B. Carroll (Cambridge, MA: MIT Press, 1956).

3 Kenneth Rexroth, *Assays* (Norfolk, CT: J. Laughlin, 1961), 27.

4 The actual words, phrases, and statements cited in this chapter have been compiled from research carried out on adolescent language by the research team mentioned in the preface.

5 Neil Howe and William Strauss, *Millennials Rising: The Next Great Generation* (New York: Vintage Books, 2000).

6 Marcel Danesi, *Cool: The Signs and Meanings of Adolescence* (Toronto: University of Toronto Press, 1994), 96.

7 Since the 1960s there has been a considerable amount of research conducted by linguists on adolescent language. I mention a few of the studies here as cases in point: C. Adelman, 'The Language of Teenage Groups,' in S. Rogers (ed.), *They Don't Speak Our Language* (London: Edward Arnold, 1976), 80–105; M.H. Leona, 'An Examination of Adolescent Clique Language in a Suburban Secondary School,' *Adolescence* 13 (1978): 495–502; W. Labov, 'Social Structure and Peer Terminology in a Black Adolescent Gang,' *Language in Society* 11 (1982): 391–413; M. Nippold (ed.), *Later Language Development* (Boston: Little, Brown and Company, 1988): P. Eckert, 'Adolescent Social Structure and the Spread of Linguistic Change,' *Language in Society* 17 (1988), 183–207; D. Eder, 'Serious and Playful Disputes: Variation on Conflict Talk among Female Adolescents,' in D. Grimshaw (ed.), *Conflict Talk* (Cambridge: Cambridge University Press, 1990), 67–84; W. Labov, 'Social Language Boundaries among Adolescents,' *American Speech* 67

(1992): 339–66; D. Cameron, 'Naming of Parts: Gender, Culture, and Terms for the Penis among American College Students,' *American Speech* 67 (1992): 367–82; Connie Eble, *Slang and Sociability* (Chapel Hill: University of North Carolina Press, 1996); T. Dalzell, *Flappers 2 Rappers: American Youth Slang* (Springfield, MA: Merriam-Webster, 1996); M. Ellis, *Slanguage: A Cool, Fresh, Phat, and Shagadelic Guide to All Kinds of Slang* (New York: Hyperion, 2000); M. Bucholtz, 'Language and Youth Culture,' *American Speech* 75 (2000): 280–3; T.C. Cooper, 'Does It Suck? or Is It for the Birds? Native Speaker Judgment of Slang Expressions,' *American Speech* 76 (2001): 62–78; J.P. Gee, A-R. Allen, and K. Clinton, 'Language, Class, and Identity: Teenagers Fashioning Themselves through Language,' *Linguistics and Education* 12 (2001): 175–94.

8   Elizabeth Hardwick, *Bartleby in Manhattan and Other Essays* (New York: Random House, 1968), 46.

9   *New York Times*, 13 February 1959, 25.

10   For a similar finding, see G. Andersen, *Pragmatic Markers and Sociolinguistic Variation: A Relevance-Theoretic Approach to the Language of Adolescents* (Amsterdam: John Benjamins, 2001); and Muffy Siegel, 'Like: The Discourse Particle and Semantics,' *Journal of Semantics* 19 (2002): 35–71.

11   This point has been made persuasively by Connie Eble in her insightful book *Slang and Sociability*.

12   Danesi, *Cool*, 105–6.

13   Alice Deignan, 'Metaphors of Desire,' in Keith Harvey and Celia Shalom (eds), *Language and Desire* (London: Routledge, 1997), 41.

14   As Raymond W. Gibbs, Jr, found in 'Irony in Talk among Friends,' *Metaphor and Symbol* 15 (2000): 5–27, irony is a strategic ploy among friends that serves specific social interactive needs.

15   Marshall McLuhan, *The Gutenberg Galaxy* (Toronto: University of Toronto Press, 1962).

16   See, for instance, Gianrenzo P. Clivio and Marcel Danesi, *The Sounds, Forms, and Uses of Italian: An Introduction to Italian Linguistics* (Toronto: University of Toronto Press, 2000), 183–7.

17   See Augusta Forconi, *La mala lingua. Dizionario dello 'slang' italiano* (Milan: Sugarco, 1988); Roberto Giacomelli, *Lingua rock. L'italiano dopo il recente costume giovanile* (Naples: Morano, 1988); M. De Paoli, *Il linguaggio del rock italiano* (Ravenna: Longo, 1988); Emanuele Banfi and Alberto A. Sobrero (eds), *Il linguaggio giovanile degli anni Novanta. Regole, invenzioni, gioco* (Bari: Laterza, 1992); Edgar Radtke (ed.), *La lingua dei giovani* (Tubingen: Narr, 1993); Claudio Giovanardi, 'Note sul linguaggio dei giovani romani di borgata,' *Studi Linguistici Italiani* 19 (1993), 62–78; Renzo Titone (ed.), *Come parlano gli*

adolescenti (Rome: Armando, 1996); Gian Ruggero Manzoni, *Peso vero sclero.*
Dizionario del linguaggio giovanile di fine millennio (Milan: Il Saggiatore, 1997).

18 W. Labov, 'Social Language Boundaries among Adolescents,' 340.

19 Peter Shaffer, *Amadeus* (London: Penguin, 1993), 108.

20 William James, *Principles of Psychology*, vol. 1 (New York: Holt, 1890), 331.

21 Oscar Wilde, 'The American Invasion,' *Court and Society Review* (London) 23
    March 1887, 11.

22 William Burroughs, *The Adding Machine* (New York: Seaver, 1985), 22.

Chapter 4. Grooving like Teenagers

1 Quoted in Simon Frith, *Sound Effects: Youth, Leisure and the Politics of Rock*
    (London: Constable, 1983), 77.

2 See, on this point, Marcus Boon, *The Road of Excess: A History of Writers on
    Drugs* (Cambridge, MA: Harvard University Press, 2002).

3 Tara Parker-Pope, *Cigarettes: Anatomy of an Industry from Seed to Smoke* (New
    York: New Press, 2001), 168.

4 Robert R. Provine, *Laughter: A Scientific Investigation* (Harmondsworth: Pen-
    guin, 2000), 205–6.

5 *New York Times*, 3 November 2002, 27.

6 Mark Gavreau Judge, *If It Ain't Got That Swing: The Rebirth of Grown-up Cul-
    ture* (New York: Spence, 2000).

7 Quoted in *Rolling Stone*, December 1990, 45.

8 Much has been written on the history and importance of pop music in the
    evolution of modern culture. In most of the writings, however, I sense an
    ambiguity about its true value as art – an ambiguity that is not found in
    critical writings on classical music. See, for instance, Robert Palmer, *Rock
    and Roll: An Unruly History* (New York: Harmony Books, 1995); D. Szat-
    mary, *A Time to Rock: A Social History of Rock 'n' Roll* (New York: Schirmer
    Books, 1996); N. George, *Hip Hop America* (New York: Viking, 1998); J.A.
    Jackson, *American Bandstand: Dick Clark and the Making of a Rock 'n' Roll
    Empire* (Oxford: Oxford University Press, 1998); Simon Reynolds, *Generation
    Ecstasy: Into the World of Techno and Rave Culture* (London: Routledge, 1999);
    A. Light (ed.), *The Vibe History of Hip Hop* (New York: Three Rivers Press,
    1999); James Miller, *Flowers in the Dustbin: The Rise of Rock and Roll, 1947–
    1977* (New York: Simon and Schuster, 1999); R. Padel, *I'm a Man: Sex, Gods
    and Rock 'n' Roll* (London: Faber and Faber, 2000).

9 George Steiner, *In Bluebeard's Castle* (London: Faber and Faber, 1971), 245.

10 Donald Roberts and Peter Christenson, *It's Not Only Rock and Roll: Popular
    Music in the Lives of Adolescents* (New York: Hampton Press, 1998).

11 R. Holloway, *All Shook Up* (New York: Spence, 2001).

12 Stephen Davis, *Old Gods Almost Dead: The 40-Year Odyssey of the Rolling Stones* (New York: Broadway, 2001).

13 John Strausbaugh, *Rock 'Til You Drop* (London: Verso, 2001).

14 Greil Marcus, *Mystery Train* (New York: E.P. Dutton, 1975), 18.

15 Henri-Frédéric Amiel, *Journal in Time* (1882; translated by Mrs Humphry Ward, 1892), entry for 17 December 1856.

Chapter 5. Time to Grow Up

1 Hermann Hesse, *Magister Ludi* (New York: Ungar, 1949).

2 Todd Gitlin, *Media Unlimited: How the Torrent of Images and Sounds Overwhelms Our Lives* (New York: Metropolitan Books, 2001).

3 Eric Hoffer, *Reflections on the Human Condition* (New York: Harper and Row, 1973), 12.

4 A good account of the kinds of problems that persist can be found in E. Burkett's *Another Planet* (New York: HarperCollins, 2001).

5 Henry Miller, *The Wisdom of the Heart* (New York: New Directions, 1941), 9.

6 Rachel Simmons, *Odd Girl Out: The Hidden Culture of Aggression in Girls* (New York: Harcourt, 2001).

7 Terri Apter, *The Myth of Maturity* (New York: W.W. Norton and Company, 2001).

8 From Neil Howe and William Strauss, *Millennials Rising: The Next Great Generation* (New York: Vintage Books, 2000), 84.

9 James Q. Wilson, *The Marriage Problem: How Our Culture Has Weakened Families* (New York: HarperCollins, 2002).

10 C.H. Cooley, *Social Organization* (New York: Scribner, 1909).

11 For a panorama of family and adolescent trends across the world, see B. Brown, R. Larson, and T.S. Saraswathi, *The World's Youth: Adolescence in Eight Regions of the Globe* (New York: Cambridge University Press, 2002); and J. Mortimer, and R. Larson (eds), *The Changing Adolescent Experience: Societal Trends and the Transition to Adulthood* (New York: Cambridge University Press, 2002).

12 Louise Bogan, *Selected Criticism: Poetry and Prose* (Chicago: H. Regnery, 1955), 89.

13 See, for instance, Glen O. Gabbard, *The Psychology of 'The Sopranos': Love, Death, Desire and Betrayal in America's Favorite Gangster Family* (New York: Basic, 2002); and Maurice Yacowar, *The Sopranos on the Couch: Analyzing Television's Greatest Series* (New York: Continuum, 2002).

14 See, on this point, Robert N. Butler, *Why Survive? Being Old in America* (New

York: Harper Torchbooks, 1974); Jack Levin and William C. Levin, *Ageism: Prejudice and Discrimination against the Elderly* (Belmont, CA: Wadsworth Publishing, 1980); Frank Nuessel, *The Semiotics of Ageism* (Toronto: Toronto Semiotic Circle Publications, 1992), and *The Image of Older Adults in the Media* (Westport, CT: Greenwood Press, 1992); and Erdman B. Palmore, *Ageism: Negative and Positive* (New York: Springer, 1999).

15 In *Fast Girls: Teenage Tribes and the Myth of the Slut* (New York: Scribner, 2001), E. White has documented that even girls as young as eight years of age are worried about being fat – a mind-set that persists through the teen years and well into adulthood. Appearance junkies, White claims, are made, not born. Our economic system and the mass distribution of images work together to make the body the primary project in the lives of too many people, especially women.

16 Karl Marx, *Economic and Philosophical Manuscripts*, 1844, trans. by R. Livingstone and G. Benton (Harmondsworth: Penguin, 1975).

17 Émile Durkheim, *Suicide: A Study in Sociology*, 1897, trans. 1952 by J.A. Spaulding and G. Simpson (London: Routledge and Kegan Paul, 1975); see also N. Rotenstreich, *Alienation: The Concept and Its Reception* (London: Brill, 1989).

18 Thomas Hine, *The Rise and Fall of the American Teenager* (New York: Bard Books, 1999). The fact that there has been a dramatic rise in violence in the schools seems to support Hine's view. See, for example, M. Miller, *Coping with Weapons and Violence in Your School and on Your Streets* (New York: Rosen Publishing Group, 1993); and S.U. Spina (ed.), *Smoke and Mirrors: The Hidden Context of Violence in Schools and Society* (Lanham, MD: Rowman and Littlefield, 2000).

19 Robert Burns, 'To a Mouse on Turning Her Up in Her Nest with the Plough' (ll. 39–42), in his *Complete Poems and Songs*, ed. by James Kinsley (Oxford: Oxford University Press, 1969).

20 Émile Durkheim, *The Elementary Forms of Religious Life* (New York: Collier, 1912).

21 For a detailed synthesis of the themes and plots on the show, see Kathleen Tracy, *The Girl's Got Bite: The Unofficial Guide to Buffy's World* (Los Angeles: Renaissance Books, 1998).

22 See also Apter, *The Myth of Maturity*.

23 Steven Pinker, *The Blank Slate: The Modern Denial of Human Nature* (New York: Viking, 2002).

24 Reported by *Newsweek*, 7 October 2002, 54.

25 L.L. Cavalli-Sforza and F. Cavalli-Sforza, *The Great Human Diasporas: The History of Diversity and Evolution* (Reading, MA: Addison-Wesley, 1995).

26 Howe and Strauss, *Millennials Rising*.
27 A view cogently argued as well by Frank Furedi, *Paranoid Parenting: Why Ignoring the Experts May Be Best for Your Child* (Chicago: Chicago Review Press, 2002).
28 Kalle Lasn, *Culture Jam: The Uncooling of America* (New York: Morrow, 2000).
29 Thomas Frank, *One Market under God* (New York: Anchor, 2000); Naomi Klein, *No Logo: Taking Aim at the Brand Bullies* (Toronto: Alfred A. Knopf, 2000).
30 See, on this point, the excellent work by J.H. Plumb, *The Penguin Book of the Renaissance* (Harmondsworth: Penguin, 1964).
31 Oscar Wilde, *The Picture of Dorian Gray* (Harmondsworth: Penguin, 1949).
32 Abba Eban, Speech, 16 December 1970, London.

Index